SHARE PRICE CHANGING FACTORS

JOHN LOK

Contents

Preface

Introduction

Share market is often changing. Share price will often change due to market environment factor influence, e.g. competitors, strategy change, reorganization, sale growth or reducing etc. different factors. How share buyers can predict share price whether it will rise or reduce in short time.

In this book, I shall indicate some external environment factors and company internal environment factors to explain how and why they will possible influence any company share price changes more easily. Readers can learn some useful knowledge to attempt to predict whether these factors can influence share price changes more easily in possible. Evaluation to any shares prices why and how and when they change, you can have more confidence to earn share profit in investment market.

Prologue

Table of content

ONE

FUNDAMENTAL ANALYSIS PAST SHARE VALUE ELEMENT EVALUATION METHOD

Fundamental analysis

Fundamental Analysts are concerned with the company that underlies the stock itself. They evaluate a company's past performance as well as the credibility of its accounts. Many performance ratios are created that aid the fundamental analyst with assessing the validity of a stock, such as the P/E ratio.

What fundamental analysis in stock market is trying to

achieve, is finding out the true value of a stock, which then can be compared with the value it is being traded with on stock markets and therefore finding out whether the stock on the market is undervalued or not. Finding out the true value can be done by various methods with basically the same principle. The principle being that a company is worth all of its future profits added together. These future profits also have to be discounted to their present value. This principle goes along well with the theory that a business is all about profits and nothing else. Contrary to technical analysis, fundamental analysis is thought of more as a long-term strategy.

Fundamental analysis is built on the belief that human society needs capital to make progress and if a company operates well, it should be rewarded with additional capital and result in a surge in stock price. Fundamental analysis is widely used by fund managers as it is the most reasonable, objective and made from publicly available information like financial statement analysis.

Another meaning of fundamental analysis is beyond bottom-up company analysis, it refers to top-down analysis from first analyzing the global economy, followed by country analysis and then sector analysis, and finally the company level analysis.

The first method is to evaluate the company basic share price , such as stock value, then to predict its future share price whether it's share price will rise up maximum price level or it's share price will fall down maximum price level in order to predict its share price variation level in general. It has four basic elements of stock value, it can be used to predict share price will rise up or fall down, they include: The Price-to-Book Ratio (P/B) ,

Price-to-Earnings Ratio (P/E) ,The PEG Ratio Dividend Yield

and The Bottom Line
Investing has a set of four basic elements that investors use to break down a stock's value. In this article, we will look at four commonly used ratios and what they can tell you about a stock. Financial ratios are powerful tools to help summarize financial statements and the health of a company or enterprise.

·Financial statements can be used by analysts and investors to compute financial ratios that indicate the health or value of a company and its shares.
·P/E, P/B, PEG and dividend yields are four commonly used metrics that can help break down a stock's value and outlook.
·Any single ratio is too narrowly focused to stand alone, so combining these and other financial ratios gives a more complete picture.

(1) The Price-to-Book Ratio (P/B)
Made for glass-half-empty people, the price-to-book (P/B) ratio represents the value of the company if it is torn up and sold today. This is useful to know because many companies in mature industries falter in terms of growth, but can still be a good value based on their assets. The book value usually includes equipment, buildings, land and anything else that can be sold, including stock holdings and bonds. With financial firms, the book value can fluctuate with the market as these stocks tend to have a portfolio of assets that goes up and down in value. Industrial companies tend to have a book value based more in physical assets, which depreciate year over year according to accounting rules. In either case, a low P/B ratio can protect you – but only if it's accurate. This means an investor has to look deeper into the

actual assets making up the ratio.

(2) Price-to-Earnings Ratio (P/E)

The price to earnings (P/E) ratio is possibly the most accurate of all the ratios. If sudden increases in a stock's price , then the P/E ratio is the steak. A stock can go up in value without significant earnings increases, but the P/E ratio is what decides if it can stay up. Without earnings to back up the price, a stock will eventually fall back down.

The reason for this is simple: A P/E ratio can be thought of as how long a stock will take to pay back your investment if there is no change in the business. A stock trading at $10 per share with earnings of $5 per share has a P/E ratio of 2, which is sometimes seen as meaning that you'll make your money back in long years if nothing changes.

The reason stocks tend to have high P/E ratios is that investors try to predict which stocks will enjoy progressively larger earnings. An investor may buy a stock with a P/E ratio of 30 if he or she thinks it will double its earnings every year (shortening the payoff period significantly). If this fails to happen, the stock will fall back down to a more reasonable P/E ratio. If the stock does manage to double earnings, then it will likely continue to trade at a high P/E ratio.

(3) The PEG Ratio

Because the P/E ratio isn't enough in and of itself, many investors use the price to earnings growth (PEG) ratio. Instead of merely looking at the price and earnings, the PEG ratio incorporates the historical growth rate of the company's earnings. This ratio also tells you how your stock stacks up against another stock. The PEG ratio is calculated by taking the P/E ratio of a company and dividing it by the

year-over-year growth rate of its earnings. The lower the value of your PEG ratio, the better the deal you're getting for the stock's future estimated earnings.
By comparing two stocks using the PEG, you can see how much you're paying for growth in each case. A PEG of 1 means you're breaking even if growth continues as it has in the past. A PEG of 2 means you're paying twice as much for projected growth when compared to a stock with a PEG of 1. This is speculative because there is no guarantee that growth will continue as it has in the past. The P/E ratio is a snap shot of where a company is and the PEG ratio is a graph plotting where it has been. Armed with this information, an investor has to decide whether it is likely to continue in that direction.

Dividend Yield
It's always nice to have a back-up when a stock's growth . This is why dividend-paying stocks are attractive to many investors – even when prices drop, you get a paycheck. The dividend yield shows how much of a payday you're getting for your money. By dividing the stock's annual dividend by the stock's price, you get a percentage. You can think of that percentage as the interest on your money, with the additional chance at growth through the appreciation of the stock.
Although , there are some things to watch for with the dividend yield. Inconsistent dividends or suspended payments in the past mean that the dividend yield can't be counted on. Whether dividend payments have increased year over year – is essential to making the decision to buy. Dividends also vary by industry, with utilities and some banks typically paying a lot whereas tech firms invest almost all their earnings back into the company to fuel

growth.

(4) The Bottom Line

P/E, P/B, PEG and dividend yields are too narrowly focused to stand alone as a single measure of a stock. By combining these methods of valuation, you can get a better view of a stock's worth. Any one of these can be influenced by creative accounting – as can more complex ratios like cash flow. As you add more tools to your valuation methods, discrepancies get easier to spot. These four main ratios may be overshadowed by thousands of customized metrics, but they will always be useful stepping stones for finding out whether a stock is worth buying.

Day traders often find themselves with complex technical indicators, moving averages, and complex algorithms. However, sometimes it helps to step back and get back to the basics. One of those basic indicators is volume (the number of shares bought and sold in any given day). As long as there has been trading, investors have used volume to get a read on where stocks are headed. And unlike most of the tools technical analysts use, this one is easily found on almost any financial Web site or in any daily newspaper with stock tables (usually expressed in thousands of shares).

However, a trader can't be depended by any one indicator. But understanding volume can provide insight into a stock's behavior to help you determine its overall health. The most important rule is this: volume precedes price. Typically, before a stock price moves, volume comes into play. The beauty of this indicator is its flexibility. Changes in volume can be used intra-day to determine short-term price movement or over several days to determine a stock's two to three day trend direction.

Before learning how to interpret volume, you have to know what is calculated. The first step is to identify a stock's typical trading range. Active traders were once relegated to writing down the volumes each day for their favorite stocks and then calculating the averages themselves. The Internet has made such information available to any investor online. Free data is available from hundreds of sites like Yahoo Finance. It will give you the average volume on any stock you choose.

In general, a price change on relatively low volume for a particular stock suggests an aberration, whereas a price change on high volume portends a genuine trend reversal. An active trader looks at volume to determine a price trend and the obvious goal is to trade in the direction of the major price trend. One of the best times to buy is when a stock is going down on low volume (with no news) as compared to recent increases on higher volume. This suggests that the selling is lighter and that the holders of the stock that are going to sell have finished selling and the rest are holding. The sellers of the stocks then may come back into the market when they see the price stabilize. It's also not a bad idea to sell on high volume on the way up (if the volume appears to be tapering off), as this usually creates abnormally high prices that cannot be maintained very long. The basic theory is this: if price and volume are moving in the same direction, the trend of the stock price will continue. If they are running counter to each other, the trend will reverse.

It's also a good sign when a share-price jump is joined by soaring volume or if declines occur on low volume. The idea is that light volume signifies little urgency, so a share-price decline probably wasn't the result of any major bad news. Low volume linked to a share-price increase is also a negative sign, because any lasting upward price movement should be confirmed with increasing volume. The worst-case scenario is high trading volume coupled with a falling share price. Volume should never be used independent of price action to determine buying or selling patterns, but it is an invaluable tool to gain insight into the markets and determine the current price trend. Hence, share buyer can apply the four basic share price elements to attempt to predict share price variation in share purchase and sale market.

Technical analysis international market competition predicts share price variation

Technical analysis

Technical analysts are not concerned with any of the company's fundamentals. They seek to determine the future price of a stock based solely on the trends of the past price (a form of time series analysis). Technical analysis is rather used for short-term strategies, than the long-term ones. And therefore, it is far more prevalent in commodities and forex markets where traders focus on short-term price movements. There are some basic assumptions used in this analysis, first being that everything significant about a company is already priced into the stock, other being that the price moves in trends and lastly that history (of prices) tends to repeat itself which is mainly because of the market psychology.

- What are the Ways To Predict Market Performance

This widely quoted piece of stock market wisdom warns investors not to get in the way of market trends. The assumption is that the best bet about market movements is that they will continue in the same direction. This concept has is roots in behavioral finance. With so many stocks to choose from, why would investors keep their money in a stock that's falling, as opposed to one that's climbing? It's classic fear and greed. Studies have found that mutual fund inflows are positively correlated with market returns. Momentum plays a part in the decision to invest and when more people invest, the market goes up, encouraging even more people to buy. It's a positive feedback loop.

(1) Reversion

Experienced investors, who have seen many market ups and downs, often take the view that the market will even out, over time. Historically, high market prices often discourage these investors from investing, while historically low prices may represent an opportunity.

The tendency of a variable, such as a stock price, to converge on an average value over time is called mean reversion. The phenomenon has been found in several economic indicators, which are useful to know, including exchange rates, gross domestic product (GDP) growth, interest rates and unemployment. Mean reversion may also be responsible for business cycles.

Some studies show mean reversion in some data sets over some periods, but many others do not. A serious obstacle in detecting mean reversion is the absence of reliable long-term series, especially because mean-reversion, if it exists, is thought to be slow and can only be picked up over long horizons." Given that academia has access to at least 80 years of stock market research, this suggests that if the market does have a tendency to mean revert, it is a phenomenon that happens slowly and almost imperceptibly, over many years or even decades.

(2) Martingales

Another possibility is that past returns just don't matter. In 1965, Paul Samuelson studied market returns and found that past pricing trends had no effect on future prices and reasoned that in an efficient market, there should be no such effect. His conclusion was that market prices are martingales.

A martingale is a mathematical series in which the best prediction for the next number is the current number. The concept is used in probability theory, to estimate the results of random motion. For example, suppose that you have $50 and bet it all on a coin toss. How much money will you have after the toss? You may have $100 or more or you may have $0 after the toss, but statistically, the best prediction is $50 -- your original starting position. The prediction of your fortunes after the toss is a martingale.

In stock option pricing, stock market returns could be assumed to be martingales. According to this theory, the valuation of the option does not depend on the past pricing trend, or on any estimate of future price trends. The current price and the estimated volatility are the only stock-specific inputs.

A martingale in which the next number is more likely to be higher is known as a sub-martingale. In popular literature, this motion is known as a random walk with upward drift. This description is consistent with the more than 80 years of stock market pricing history. Despite many short-term reversals, the overall trend has been consistently higher. If stock returns are essentially random, the best prediction for tomorrow's market price is simply today's price, plus a very small increase. Rather than focusing on past trends and looking for possible momentum or mean reversion, investors should instead concentrate on managing the risk inherent in their volatile investments.

(3) The Search for Value

Value investors purchase stock cheaply and expect to be

rewarded later. Their hope is that an inefficient market has underpriced the stock, but that the price will adjust over time. The question is: Does this happen, and why would an inefficient market make this adjustment?

Research suggests this mispricing and readjustment consistently happens, although it presents very little evidence for why it happens. Some share researchers indicate the three-factor model to explain stock market prices. The most significant factor in explaining future price returns was valuation as measured by the price-to-book ratio (P/B). Stocks with low price-to-book ratios delivered significantly better returns than other stocks.

Valuation ratios tend to move results for stocks with low price-earnings (P/E) ratios. Since then, the same effect has been found in many other studies across dozens of markets. However, studies have not explained why the market is consistently mispricing these "value" stocks and then adjusting later. The only conclusion that could be drawn is that these stocks have extra risk, for which investors demand additional compensation for taking extra risk.

Price is the driver of the valuation ratios, therefore, the findings do support the idea of a mean-reverting stock market. As prices climb, the valuation ratios get higher and, as a result, future predicted returns are lower. However, the market P/E ratio has fluctuated widely over time and has never been a consistent buy or sell signal.

(4) The Bottom Line

Even after decades of study by the brightest minds in finance, there are no solid answers. The only conclusion that can be drawn is that there may be some momentum effects, in the short term and a weak mean-reversion effect, in the long term. The current price is a key component of valuation ratios such as P/B and P/E, that have been shown to have some predictive power on the future returns of a stock. However, these ratios should not be viewed as specific buy and sell signals, but as factors that have been shown to play a role in increasing or reducing the expected long-term return.

(5) Initiation Price Changes reflect the company will change share price as soon as possible

Companies are bound to face market situations where they are required to initiate price changes. It means, either they are to cut the prices or increase the present prices to survive, maintain status quo or further growth. Initiating price changes involves two possibilities of price cuts and price increases.

Initiating Price Cuts:

There are good many circumstances where a firm is to resort to price cuts. There are genuine reasons for cutting prices:

First may be existence of excess capacity. In such situation the firm is badly in need of additional business and cannot generate it through increased sales efforts, product improvement or even price rise. It may resort to aggressive pricing, but in initiating price out, the company may trigger a price war. Second reason for initiating price cut is a drive to dominate the market through lower costs, either the company starts with lower costs than its competitors or it initiates price cuts in the hope of gaining the market share and lower costs to price cutting policy involves the following possible reasons:

1. Low-quality reason:

Consumers will assume that quality is low.

2. Fragile-market share reason:

A low price buys market share but not market loyalty. The same customers will shift to any lower- priced firm that comes along.

3. Shallow-pockets reason:

The higher priced competitors may cut their prices and may have longer staying power because of deeper cash resources.

(6) Initiating Price Increases:

Price increase is a source of maximizing the profit or maintaining it if done carefully. Say a company earns 5 percent profit on sales, and one percent price increase will increase profits by 55 per cent if sales volume is not affected.

The factors leading to price increase can be:

1. Increase in cost inflation. That is rising costs unmatched by productivity gains squeeze profit margins and lead companies to regular rounds of price increases. Companies often raise their by more than the cost hike, in anticipation of further inflation or government price controls, in a practice called anticipatory pricing.

2. Over demand can be another cause that leads to price increase. When the company cannot supply all of its customers, it can raise its prices, ration or cut supplies to customers or both.

The price can be increased by at least four ways:

1. Delayed quotation pricing:

Here, the company does not set final price until product is finished or delivered. This pricing is prevalent in industries with long production lead times like construction and heavy industrial equipment.

2. Unbundling:

The company under this plan maintains its price but removes or prices separately one or more elements that were part of the former offer, such as free delivery or installation. Automobile companies, sometimes, add antilock brakes and passenger-side air-bags as supplementary extras to their whiles.

3. Escalator clauses:
Under this, the company asks the customer to pay today's price and all or part of any inflation increase that takes place before delivery. This hike based on specified price index. These escalation clauses are quite common in construction line whether it is a house or industrial project or air-craft and ship building.

4. Reduction of discounts:
The company asks the sales force to offer its normal cash and quantity discounts at reduced rate. To gain four such attempts, the company must avoid looking like a price gouger. Companies also think of who will bear the brunt of the increased prices. It is so because, customer memories are long, and they can turn against the company which is perceived as price variation

(7) Reactions to Price Changes:
Naturally any price change provokes response or reaction from customers, competitors, distributors and suppliers and even the government. Here, we shall touch only the reactions of consumers and competitors.

Customer Reactions:
Consumers are more interested in knowing the cause or causes of price change.

A price cut can be interpreted in several ways:

1. The item or product is about to be replaced by a new model.
2. The item is faulty and it is not selling well.
3. The firm's financial position is badly affected.

4. The price will come down further.
5. The quality has been reduced.

A price may have some positive meanings:

1. The items is 'hot' sale
2. It has a high value because of quality.

Competitor Reactions:

Competitors are most likely to react when the number of firms is few, the product is homogeneous, and buyers are highly informed. Competitor reactions can be a special problem when they have a strong value proposition. The price hike them to take steps based on objectives of such price hike where they will resort to advertising and product improving efforts.

In case of price cuts, they have different interpretations:

1. That the company's trying to steal the market
2. That the company is doing poorly and trying to boost its sales
3. That company wants the whole industry to reduce prices to stimulate total demand.

So technical analysis method is one customer psychological prediction method to evaluate whether the products will be popular to sell to the market in order to predict whether the company share price will rise up or fall down.

TWO

MARKET MIMICRY

Using new statistical analysis tools of complexity theory, it performed research on predicting stock market crashes. It has long been thought that market crashes complex that may or may not be justified by external news. This research indicates that it is the internal structure of the market, not external crises, which is primarily responsible for crashes. The number of different stocks that move up or down together were shown to be an indicator of the mimicry within the market, how much investors look to one another for cues. When the mimicry is high, many stocks follow each other's movements . It was shown that a dramatic increase in market mimicry occurred during the entire year before each market crash of the past 25 years, including the financial crisis of 2007–08.

- Applying Trade war threatens counter measure to tariffs to predict whether how influences share price variation

A trade war is when a nation imposes tariffs or quotas on imports and foreign countries retaliate with similar forms of trade protectionism. As it escalates, a trade war reduces international trade. A trade war starts when a nation attempts to protect its domestic industry and create jobs. In the short run, it may work. Tariffs are supposed to give a competitive advantage to domestic producers of that product. Their prices would be lower by comparison. As a result, they would receive more orders from local customers. As their businesses grow, they would add jobs. But in the long run, a trade war costs jobs. It depresses economic growth for all countries involved. It also triggers inflation when tariffs increase the prices of imports.

Smoot-Hawley was designed to support U.S. farmers who had been ravaged by the Dust Bowl. But it also raised food prices for Americans who were already suffering from the Great Depression. Other countries retaliated with their own tariffs. The trade war reduced international trade by 65%. It turned a recession into a depression and contributed to the start of World War II. After World War II, it influences many international companies' share prices to be fallen down, due to global economy is worse.

- Trump's Trade Wars how to influence share price.

US Trading Statistic indicated that President Donald Trump wants to reduce the $621 billion U.S. trade deficit. It's been the world's largest since 1975. Reducing the deficit is part of Trump's strategy to create more jobs in US. By US trading statistic , it indicates that most of the U.S. deficit results from American enthusiasm for imported consumer products and automobiles. In 2018, the United States imported $648 billion in drugs, televisions, clothing, and other household items. It only exported $206 billion of these consumer goods. That alone added $442 billion to the deficit. America imported $372 billion worth of automobiles and parts, while only exporting $159 billion. That added another $214 billion to the trade deficit.

In early 2018, Trump said, "Trade wars are good and easy to win." He has initiated three: a global tariff on steel, a tariff on European autos, and tariffs on Chinese imports. After Trump's announcement, global stock markets tumbled in fear of a trade war between the world's three largest economies. In late 2018, several U.S. companies formed "Tariffs Hurt the Heartland." They are hurt by the rising costs of imported materials. The Federal Reserve estimates Trump's tariffs are costing the average American household $1,245 a year. This includes higher prices and lost economic growth.

US trading statistic also indicated that farmers suffer from retaliatory tariffs imposed by China and Europe on their exports. In the farm belt of Illinois, Indiana, and Wisconsin, bankruptcies have risen to their highest level in a decade. In 2017, those states produced half of all U.S. food. Nationally, farmers' income fell by $11.8 billion between January and March 2019. That's the most since 2016. On May 23, 2019, Trump gave farmers $16 billion in aid to partially compensate for their losses. He gave them $12 billion in 2018. Other countries are forming trade agreements excluding the United States. In April 2018, the EU upgraded its agreement with Mexico, removing almost all tariffs. In July 2018, the EU signed an agreement with Japan that reduces or ends tariffs on almost all goods. It's the largest bilateral trade agreement in existence, covering $152 billion in goods.

- Steel Tariffs how to influence global steel manufacturing industry price variation

US trading Statistic also indicated that on March 8, 2018, Trump administration announced a 25% tariff on steel and a 10% tariff on aluminum imports. It said that dependence on imported metals threatens America's ability to make weapons. The Aerospace Industry Council said Trump's tariffs would raise the military's costs instead. The U.S. Congress is the only body authorized to impose tariffs. But in 1962, it allowed the president to curb imports that threatened national security. The World Trade Organization can't adjudicate trade disputes that involve security.

US Trading statistic indicated that in the past, America is the world's largest steel importer, thanks to users like automakers. Steel importers employ 6.5 million workers compared to 147,000 workers in the U.S. steel industry. Tariffs lowered second-quarter profits for the big three automakers. To satisfy shareholders, they passed those costs onto consumers. Costs from tariffs have already outweighed any benefits of Trump's tax plan. Eight countries filed complaints with the World Trade Organization. Six of them - Canada, India, and Mexico, the European Union, Norway, and Switzerland - pointed out they are allies. The other two complainants are China and Russia.

US Trading Statistics also indicated that on March 26, 2018, Trump exempted South Korea, Argentina, Australia, and Brazil from the steel tariff. South Korea agreed to double its import quota for U.S. cars. It allowed the United States to keep its 25% tariff on pickup trucks for an additional 20 years. After the June 11, 2018, G7 meeting, Canadian Prime Minister Justin Trudeau said Canada would retaliate with tariffs. Mexico announced tariffs on flat steel, lamps, and pork products. On May 17, 2019, Trump agreed to lift the tariffs in 48 hours on steel imports from Canada and Mexico. In return, they will prevent Chinese steel from being shipped from their countries to the United States.

Hence, it implies that Chinese steel manufacturing companies' share prices will have chance to be fallen down due to US steel import tariff raising factor, it influence its steel cost also raises and steel sale price also rises, then any steel buyers will choose to buy steel from other countries steel manufacturers. So, it will lose many shareholders' investing confidence.

- Tariffs Against Mexico how to influence Mexico companies' share price variation

US Trading Statistic indicated that on June 4, 2019, Trump threatened to impose a 5% tariff on all imports from Mexico effective June 10. He wants the government to reduce the number of asylum-seekers presenting themselves at the U.S.-Mexico border. He promised to raise the tariff to 25% if needed to force Mexico to act. The tariff would be in violation of NAFTA. Trump said he can override the trade agreement by declaring a national emergency. Republicans, who have supported the president, are threatening to oppose this latest action. So, US raising tariff to Mexico importer strategy will influence Mexico many importers whose cost rise and their products prices will raise, then it will bring customer number to be reduced in possible . Consequently, their share prices will be fallen down, due to shareholders lose confidence to invest to Mexico businesses and they will sell shares any time.

- U.S. - China Trade War Major Events Timeline to China technological and electronic and machine manufacturing industries share price influence

US Trading Statistic indicated that the largest U.S. trade deficit by country is with China. In 2018, the U.S. trade deficit with China was $419 billion. The United States imported $540 billion, primarily in computers, cell phones, and apparel. Much of this is manufactured in China by U.S. companies but is still considered imports. The U.S. companies exported $120 billion to China. Most of this was commercial aircraft, soybeans, and autos.

In addition to reducing the trade deficit, Trump wants to limit U.S. technology transfers to Chinese companies. China requires foreign companies who want to sell products in China to share their trade secrets. The administration has also asked China to stop subsidizing the 10 industries prioritized in its "Made in China 2025" plan. These include robotics, aerospace, and software. China also plans to be the world's primary artificial intelligence center by 2030. China is unlikely to agree to those demands. The Trump administration has imposed three tariffs on a total of $250 billion in Chinese imports. The Federal Reserve estimated these tariffs cost the average household $419 per year. On May 20, 2019, Trump imposed a fourth tariff. He raised tariffs to 25% on $200 billion worth of goods. The Fed estimated it would cost the average household $831 a year. Trump is increasing the pressure on trade talks that are underway.

Trump threatened to expand that tariff to an additional $325 billion of Chinese imports. That would raise prices on basically all Chinese imports. On June 29, 2019, Trump delayed the proposed tariffs to encourage renewed trade talks with China.

China imposed a 25% tariff on $60 billion of U.S. goods on June 1, 2019. Some investors are also worried China may sell some of its $1.13 trillion in U.S. debt. That would send interest rates higher and slow the U.S. economy.

US Trading Statistic indicated that these important dates announce , they can influence US and China some industries share price variation, however, US aims to let its industies shares prices can rise to benefit their industries development and the tariff strategy can influence China some industries shares prices to be fallen down because it will influence some China industries shareholders lose confidence to invest these China industries in possible. US Trading Statistic indicated that these import tariff announce dates include as below:

On January 22, 2018, President Trump imposed tariffs and quotas on imported Chinese solar panels and washing machines. China is a world leader in solar equipment manufacturing.

On March 8, 2018, Trump asked China to develop a plan to reduce the trade deficit by $100 billion. China's economic reform plan includes reducing its reliance on exports. But it said it can't stop Americans from demanding low-cost Chinese goods.

On March 22, 2018, the administration announced tariffs on $60 billion of Chinese imports. It said China uses cybertheft, espionage, and government pressure to obtain leading-edge technology. On March 23, China announced tariffs on $3 billion of U.S. fruit, pork, recycled aluminum, and steel pipes.

On March 26, 2018, the administration began negotiations with China. It asked China to reduce tariffs on U.S. automobiles, import more U.S. semiconductors, and grant greater access to its financial sector.

On April 3, 2018, the administration threatened a 25% tariff on $50 billion in Chinese electronics, aerospace, and machinery. Hours later, China announced 25% tariffs on 106 U.S. exports. On April 18, China penalized two other U.S. exports: sorghum and Boeing airplanes. It targeted industries located in states that supported Trump in the 2016 election. It lifted the sorghum tariffs on May 18.

On May 2, 2018, China canceled all U.S. soybean import contracts. China imported $12 billion in U.S. soybeans to feed pigs, its primary meat staple. It replaced U.S. beans with those from Brazil. U.S. farmers sold one-half of their crop to China. As that market disappeared, it hurt the United States more than China. In July 2018, soybean prices hit a 10-year low as analysts predicted oversupply.

On April 5, 2018, Trump threatened tariffs on $100 billion more of Chinese imports. It would cover just one-third of U.S. imports from China. If China retaliated in kind, it would slap levies on all U.S. exports to China.

On April 10, 2018, China announced it would reduce tariffs on imported vehicles. But most automakers find it's cheaper to build in China, regardless of tariffs.

On May 4, 2018, the administration asked China to reduce the trade deficit by $200 billion and cut tariffs on U.S. goods by 2020. It asked China to end subsidies to tech companies, stop stealing U.S. intellectual property, and become open to more U.S. investment.

On May 15, 2018, China agreed to allow Qualcomm to acquire NXP. In exchange, the United States would remove tariffs on Chinese telecom company ZTE.

This agreement supports a mercantilist philosophy. It promotes specific industries that are important for the leaders' political purposes.

- How US tariff strategy influences China telecom industry strategy change and share price change

US Trading Statistic indicated that the telecom industry is part of China's growth strategy, which is one reason Trump imposed tariffs. The other is that the company violated U.S. sanctions against Iran and North Korea. On June 12, the

Senate blocked Trump's deal. Many countries see Trump's removal of tariffs on ZTE as a weakness they could exploit. They will redouble efforts to find exceptions to Trump's tariffs. Many European countries want to avoid U.S. sanctions on Iran. They may threaten tariffs on U.S. imports as a bargaining tool.

On May 21, 2018, China agreed to cut tariffs on U.S. auto imports from 25% to 15%. It would go into effect July 1.

On May 29, 2018, the administration said it would target $50 billion in imports from China. It would also restrict Chinese acquisition of U.S. technology.

On July 6, 2018, U.S. tariffs went into effect for $34 billion of Chinese imports. China retaliated with a 40% tariff on U.S. autos. Tesla announced it will build a factory in Shanghai to avoid the tariff. China also announced tariffs on U.S. agricultural exports.

- How US tariff strategy influences US farming industry development

US Trading Statistic also indicated that Midwest farmers have been stuck with excess produce and livestock. On July 24, 2018, Trump announced he would offer $12 billion in subsidies to American farmers. On August 27, the administration announced a $4.7 billion bailout. Corn growers alone said their costs top $6 billion.

On July 11, 2018, the administration announced 10% tariffs on another $200 billion of Chinese imports. They went into effect in mid-September 2018, weeks before the 2018 midterm elections. The U.S. also threatened 25% tariffs after January 1, 2019, on a variety of consumer goods, including fish, luggage, tires, handbags, furniture, apparel, and mattresses.

● How US tariff strategy influences these China industries strategy and share price change

US Trading Statistic also indicated that China threatened to retaliate by adding tariffs on $60 billion in U.S. exports. In response, Trump threatened to add tariffs until all $500 billion of Chinese imports are affected. That could have reduced economic growth by 0.75 points in 2018. It might have also threatened U.S. shale oil exports. China buys 20% of U.S. oil exports. Below these important dates tariff strategy announced, they can influence China and US share prices variation as below:

On August 2, 2018, the administration announced a 25% tariff on $16 billion worth of Chinese goods. It went into effect on August 23. It applied to industrial equipment like tractors, plastic tubes, and chemicals. In response, China announced a 25% tariff on $16 billion worth of U.S. goods, including autos and coal. It went into effect the same day.

On September 18, 2018, the administration announced tariffs on $200 billion of Chinese imports. A 10% tariff would launch on September 24, 2018. It would increase to 25% on January 1, 2019. The tariffs were imposed on 5,745 items. They encompassed a wide range of electronics, food, tools, and housewares.

On December 1, 2018, President Trump met with China's President Xi Jinping at the G-20 Conference. Trump agreed to delay the 25% tariff increase from January 1, 2019, to March 1, 2019. Negotiators planned to cover 142 issues. These included the protection of intellectual property, technology, and cybersecurity, as well as currency, agriculture, and energy.

On December 11, various federal agencies said they would condemn China for stealing U.S. trade secrets and technologies. The Justice Department would indict hackers who broke into U.S. networks. Later that day, China agreed to roll back some auto tariffs raised earlier in. It also agreed to reinstate some purchases of soybean imports and allow U.S. firms greater access to Chinese industries.

On January 18, 2019, China agreed to increase its purchases of U.S. exports and reduce the trade deficit.

On February 27, 2019, the administration dropped the threat of imposing the 25% tariff. It was originally scheduled to begin January 1, then moved to March 1, then dropped.

● What factors can cause the U.S. Trade War with China

U.S. politicians have long threatened a trade war with America's largest trading partner in goods. A trade deficit occurs when exports are less than imports.

US Trading Statistic also indicated that in 2017, the United States exported $130 billion to China. The three largest export categories are aircraft at $16 billion; soybeans, $12 billion; and automobiles, $11 billion. U.S. imports from China were $506 billion. Most of it is electronics, clothing, and machinery.

Half of all Chinese imports are goods used by U.S. manufacturers to make other products. They send raw materials to China for low-cost assembly. Once shipped back to the United States, they are considered imports. The tariffs raise their costs, forcing them to either raise prices or lay off workers. An example is salmon caught in Alaska and sent to China for processing, then sent back to U.S. grocery shelves. If Trump imposes tariffs on seafood imports, it will raise prices by 25 cents to 50 cents a pound.

China is the world's No.1 exporter. Its comparative advantage is that it can produce consumer goods for lower costs than other countries can. China has a lower standard of living, which allows its companies to pay lower wages. American companies can't compete with China's low costs, so it loses U.S. manufacturing jobs. Americans, of course, want these goods for the lowest prices. Most are not willing to pay more for "Made in America."

In the battle to capture the customer, companies use a wide range of tactics to ward off competitors. Increasingly, price is the weapon of choice—and frequently the skirmishing degenerates into a price war.

Creating low-price appeal is often the goal, but the result of one retaliatory price slashing after another is often a precipitous decline in industry profits. Look at the airline price wars of 1992. When American Airlines, Northwest Airlines, and other U.S. carriers went toe-to-toe in matching and exceeding one another's reduced fares, the result was record volumes of air travel—and record losses. Some estimates suggest that the overall losses suffered by the industry that year exceed the combined profits for the entire industry from its inception.

● What are price wars influence ?

Price wars can create economically devastating and psychologically debilitating situations that take an extraordinary toll on an individual, a company, and industry profitability. No matter who wins, the combatants all seem to end up worse off than before they joined the battle. And yet, price wars are becoming increasingly common and uncommonly fierce. US Trading Statistic the following two examples to influence share price variation:

·In July 1999, Sprint announced a nighttime long-distance rate of 5 cents per minute. In August 1999, MCI matched Sprint's off-peak rate. Later that month, AT&T acknowledged that revenue from its consumer long-distance business was falling, and the company cut its long-distance rates to 7 cents per minute all day, everyday, for a monthly fee of $5.95. AT&T's stock dropped 4.7% the day of the announcement. MCI's stock price dropped 2.5%; Sprint's fell 3.8%.

•E-Trade and other electronic brokers are changing the competitive terrain of financial services with their extraordinarily low-priced brokerage services. The prevailing price for discount trades has fallen from $30 to $15 to $8 in the past few years.

There is little doubt, in the first example, that the major players in the long-distance phone business are in a price war. Price reductions, per-second billing, and free calls are the principal weapons the players bring to the competitive arena. There is little talk from any of the carriers about service, quality, brand equity, and other non price factors that might add value to a product or service. Virtually every competitive move is based on price, and every countermeasure is a retaliatory price cut.

In the second example, the competitive situation is subtly different—and yet still very much a price war. E-Trade's success demonstrates how the emergence of the Internet has fundamentally changed the cost of doing business. Consequently, even businesses such as Charles Schwab, which used to compete primarily on low-price appeal, are chanting a "quality" mantra. Meanwhile, Merrill Lynch and American Express have recognized that the emergence of the Internet will affect pricing and are changing their price structures to include free online trades for high-end customers. These companies appear to be engaged in more focused pricing battles, unlike the "globalized" price war in the long-distance phone market.

Most managers will be involved in a price war at some point

in their careers. Every price cut is potentially the first salvo, and some discounts routinely lead to retaliatory price cuts that then escalate into a full-blown price war. That's why it's a good idea to consider other options before starting a price war or responding to an aggressive price move with a retaliatory one. Often, companies can avoid a debilitating price war altogether by using a set of alternative tactics. Our goal is to describe an arsenal of weapons other than price cuts that managers who are engaged in or contemplating a price war may also want to consider.

● How price wars influence shareholders behavior

Generally, price wars start because somebody somewhere thinks prices in a certain market are too high. Or someone is willing to buy market share at the expense of current margins. Price wars are becoming more common because managers tend to view a price change as an easy, quick, and reversible action. When businesses don't trust or know one another very well, the pricing battles can escalate very quickly. And whether they play out in the physical or the virtual world, price wars have a similar set of antecedents. By understanding their causes and characteristics, managers can make sensible decisions about when and how to fight a price war, when to flee one—and even when to start one.

Price wars are becoming more common because managers tend to view a price change as an easy, quick, and reversible action. The influence steps include as below:

The first step, Consider a small commodities supplier that suddenly found that its largest competitor had slashed prices to a level well below the small company's costs. One option the smaller company considered was to lower its price in a tit-for-tat move. But that price would have been below the supplier's marginal cost; it would have suffered debilitating losses. Fortunately, a few phone calls revealed that its adversary was attempting to drive the supplier out of the local market by underpricing its products locally but maintaining high prices elsewhere. The supplier correctly diagnosed the pricing move as predatory and elected to do two things.

First, the manager called customers in the competitor's home market to let them know that the price-cutter was offering special deals in another market. Second, he called local customers and asked them for their support, pointing out that if the smaller supplier was driven off the market, its customers would be facing a monopolist. The short-term price cuts would turn into long-term price hikes. The supplier identified solutions that eschewed further price cuts and thus averted a price war.

Intelligent analysis that leads to accurate diagnosis is more than half the cure. The process emphasizes understanding the opportunities for pricing actions based on current market trends and responding to competitors' actions based on the players and their resources. Not only is it necessary to understand why a price war is occurring or may occur, it also is critical to recognize where to look for the resources to do battle.

The four key areas in the theater of operations. They are customer issues such as price sensitivity and the customer segments that may emerge if prices change; company issues such as a business's cost structures, capabilities, and strategic positioning; competitor issues, such as a rival's cost structures, capabilities, and strategic positioning; and contributor issues, or the other players in the industry whose self-interest or profiles may affect the outcome of a price war.

It's necessary to understand why a price war is

occurring—or may occur. But it's also critical to recognize where to look for resources in battle. It's important to carefully analyze your customers, company, competitors, and other players within and outside the industry that may have an interest in how the price war plays out.

● How prices war influences customers and price sensitivity

A thoughtful evaluation of customers and their price sensitivities can provide valuable insights about whether one should fight a competitor's price cut with a price cut in kind or with some other strategy. Consumers are frequently unaware of substitute products and their prices, or they may find it difficult to make comparisons among functionally equivalent alternatives. For instance, prior to AT&T's 7-cents-a-minute plan, consumers faced a bewildering set of pricing options for long-distance phone service. AT&T charged 15 cents per minute per call with no monthly fee; or 10 cents per minute with a $4.95 monthly fee. MCI offered nighttime rates of 5 cents a minute, daytime rates of up to 25 cents a minute, and a monthly fee of $1.95. Sprint charged 5 cents per minute for nighttime calls, rates of up to 10 cents per minute for other calls, and a $5.95 monthly fee. The cost of determining the best plan when customers are unsure about their calling patterns is simply too high for a low-involvement decision like long-distance phone service. A company that wanted to compete on price could choose to simplify. That's exactly what Sprint did. It simplified its price schedule to 10 cents a minute so customers could compare its rates to those from MCI and AT&T.

Some consumers are more sensitive to quality than price, for a variety of reasons. Industrial buyers are often willing to pay more for on-time delivery or consistent quality because they need those features to make their businesses run smoother and more profitably. The very rational belief that poor quality can endanger one's health is an important reason that branded drugs command the prices they do relative to generic drugs. And snob appeal allows Davidoff to sell matches at $3.25 for a box of 40 sticks to cigar connoisseurs. The basic lesson is that different customer segments exhibit different levels of price sensitivity for different products at different times. Businesses that adopt a one-size-fits-all approach to pricing do so at their peril.

- How prices war influences company abilities

Company factors such as cost structures, capabilities, and strategic positioning should also be examined carefully. Cost structures may be affected by changes in technology or business practices, which in turn may tempt a company to cut prices in a manner that will trigger a price war. For example, consider the implications of outsourcing. It's probably true that it is cheaper to buy rather than make something in-house, because the invisible hand of the marketplace will lower the acquisition price of a product. But the cost of manufacturing something in-house is largely sunk and fixed. When that product is purchased on the market, its acquisition cost is a variable one. In other words, integration can lead to a cost structure with a higher fixed-cost component and a lower variable-cost component. Consequently, the company with the lower variable costs may be tempted to reduce prices and start a price war. But even though the lower variable costs give the company an advantage, it should carefully consider whether a price war is consistent with its strategic posture. The company's lower variable costs should be used to start a price war only when it will result in the neutralization or the exit of an undesirable rival.

Consider, too, the coherence of your pricing strategy and your ability to execute it. The actions of one participant engaged in a fierce price war in the utility industry is telling: The company's senior management group asked its top manager to increase market share by 20%, return prices to profitable levels, and stabilize them. Confronted with apparently conflicting goals, the manager chose the easiest goal—build market share—which he achieved by lowering prices, thus exacerbating the price war. The directive to the manager was confusing, his resulting actions baffled competitors, and that led to considerable uncertainty and increased price turbulence in the market. When the soft costs (managerial time and attention) of changing prices through a complex supply chain were factored in, the cost of the increased market share was very dear. The essential insight that should emerge from this exercise is whether a simple price cut is the best option given one's cost structure, capacity levels, and organizational competence.

- How prices war influences competitors' response

An analysis of competitors—their cost structures, capabilities, and strategic positioning—is equally valuable. Industrywide price reductions may be appropriate under certain circumstances. But many unprofitable price wars happen because a company sees an opportunity to increase market share or profits through lower prices, while ignoring the fact that competitors will respond. Market research may reveal that sales increases following a price cut justify the action, but this same research often simply ignores competitors' price responses.

Businesses need to pay attention at the strategic level to the twin questions of who will respond and how. Smart product managers recognize the need to understand the competition and empathize with them. They project how competitors will set prices by carefully tracking historical patterns, understanding which events have triggered price changes in the past, and by tracking the timing and magnitude of price responses. They monitor public statements made by senior executives and published in company reports. And they keep their eyes peeled for activity in resource markets: competitors that acquire a new technology, labor force, information system, or distribution channel, or that form a new brand alliance, will probably make some kind of a price move that will affect other players in the industry.

A company's direct competitors that share the same technology and speak to the same markets are important rivals. But indirect competitors that satisfy customer needs through the use of different technologies and that have completely different cost structures are perhaps the most dangerous. In fact, direct competitors such as major airlines frequently coexist quite peacefully. Examining their pricing-decision rules suggests why. U.S. Department of Transportation studies indicate that when one hub-based airline enters another's hub, it typically does not engage in price-based competition because it fears retaliation in its own hub. Conversely, price wars may often be started by a company from an entirely different industry, with a radically different technology, whose cost advantages give it enough leverage to enter your market and steal your share.

The process of identifying competitors also reveals the strengths and weaknesses of current and potential rivals. This has important implications for how a company competes. It is generally wise to not stir a hornet's nest by starting a price war with a competitor that has a significantly larger resource base or a reputation for being a fierce price warrior. When analyzing your competition, carefully determine who they are, how price fits with their strategic position, how they make pricing decisions, and what their capabilities and resources are.

- How prices war influences contributors, collaborators, and other interested parties market behavioral change

Finally, it is important to monitor other players in the industry whose self-interest or profiles may affect outcomes. Suppliers, distributors, providers of complementary goods and services, customers, government agencies, and so on contribute significantly to the consumption experience, including product quality, the sales pitch, and after-sales service. They often wield considerable influence on the outcome of a price war—directly or indirectly. Sometimes these contributors may provide the impetus for, or may indirectly start, a price war. For Motorola phone company market behavioral change example, it discovered as much when it introduced low-priced cellular phones in China and Brazil. Soon Motorola observed that the street price for its phones had dropped substantially in the United States. Distributors were diverting products bound for China and Brazil to the profitable U.S. and European markets; sometimes the products never even left the dock. Motorola's distributors had created a "gray market" because Motorola had given them a reason to believe that prices in the United States were too high.

Sometimes contributors can help reduce price competition by enhancing the product's value, as Intel does for computer manufacturers; assisting with marketing, as airline frequent-flyer programs do for credit-card companies; and limiting the exposure to competing products, as MITI has done for Japanese companies facing international competition at home. Smart managers must carefully consider other players and their interests (profit margins for suppliers and distributors, commissions for sales representatives, and so on) before starting a price war or joining one.

- How to fight a Price War

Companies that step back and examine those four areas carefully often find that they actually have quite a few different options—including defusing the conflict, fighting it out on several fronts, or retreating. We'll look at some of those strategies and how companies have deployed them successfully.

Stop the War Before It Starts

There are several ways to stop a price war before it starts. One is to make sure your competitors understand the rationale behind your pricing policies. In other words, reveal your strategic intentions. Price-matching policies, everyday low pricing, and other public statements may communicate to competitors that you intend to fight a price war using all possible resources. But frequently these declarations about low prices, or about not engaging in price promotions, aren't low-price strategies at all. Such announcements are simply a way to tell competitors that you prefer to compete on dimensions other than price. When your competitors agree that such competition will be more profitable than competing on price, they'll tend to go along.

That is precisely what happened when Winn-Dixie followed the Big Star supermarket chain in North Carolina and announced that it, too, would meet or beat mutual rival

Food Lion's prices. After two years, the number of equi-priced products among 79 commonly purchased brand items at the supermarkets had more than doubled. Further, the overall market price level had increased for these products. What happened? The stores stopped competing on price. In fact, the data suggest that Food Lion raised its prices after its competitors announced they would match Food Lion's prices. Making sure that your competitors know that your costs are low is another option—one that effectively warns them about the potential consequences of a price war. Hence it sometimes pays to reveal your cost advantage..

Rather than use its low-cost structure to compete on price to build market share, Sara Lee uses its low costs as an implicit threat that helps prevent price wars. Essentially, a business that has relatively low variable costs enjoys an enviable advantage in a price war since competitors cannot sustain a price below their own variable costs in the long run. But low-cost companies should carefully consider their strategic positions before they start or join a price war. Lower costs often tempt a business to cut its prices, but doing so can diminish consumers' perceptions of quality and may trigger an unprofitable price war.

- Responding with Non price Actions

Sometimes an analysis of the market reveals that several customer segments exhibit different degrees of sensitivity to price and quality. (See the sidebar "Price Sensitivity on the Web" for a look at how managers can identify and exploit differences in customers' price sensitivities—even in an information-rich environment.) Understanding the basis for certain customers' price sensitivities lets managers creatively respond to a rival's price cut without cutting their own prices. For example, a company might be able to focus on quality, not price.

- Price Sensitivity on the Web

Internet companies such as Buy.com are attempting to build market share by charging low prices. They operate under the premise that Internet shoppers are extremely sensitive to price. But the evidence to back up that assumption is mixed. On the one hand, the Web offers an easy way to search and compare prices. That is why Amazon.com can charge higher prices than other on-line sites. The variety of titles it offers, the extensive product information it provides, and its reputation for rapid and reliable shipping make Amazon an easy choice for consumers who want convenience and low prices.

The growth of Internet shopping is posing interesting pricing dilemmas for bricks-and-mortar retailers. On-line vendors don't have to maintain a physical presence close to their customers, so they can operate out of a few large warehouses, thus lowering their costs. It would generally be unwise for bricks-and-mortar retailers to try to compete on price given the relatively high cost of maintaining a storefront. Instead, their strategy should emphasize features that can't be provided over the Web, such as personalized face-to-face service, browsing, immediate delivery, low-hassle returns and exchanges that don't require repackaging and shipping, and the ability to touch the product. Several retailers, such as Barnes & Noble and Tower Records, have developed an Internet presence to complement their store-fronts. Such "clicks and mortar" retailers give customers the option to purchase or order on-line and then pick up the product at a bricks-and-mortar branch, and those retailers often provide a search engine in the store that is similar to their Internet offerings. Finally, a keen understanding of consumer behavior lets some companies charge higher prices on the Web because of the anonymity that on-line transactions offer. In a recent study of 46 e-tailers of prescription drugs, the two most popular items (Viagra, a medication for erectile dysfunction, and Propecia, a medication to treat male pattern baldness) were priced roughly 10% higher than in drug stores. For obvious reasons, people prefer to have those prescriptions filled without personal contact and are willing to pay a premium for a faceless transaction.

For Malaysian travelling entertainment industry influence, the economic turmoil dramatically reduced the value of the Malaysian ringgit to about half its value a few years earlier. The cost of a hotel room plummeted along with the nose-diving currency, yet hotel rooms went a-begging. What did the luxury hotel operators do to attract customers? They dropped their room rates even further. Luxury hotels in Malaysia entered a price war. All but one.

When luxury hotels start cutting their guest rates, their ability to offer "luxury" accoutrements drops. US Trading Statistic indicated that that means no fresh flowers, fewer towels, and a noticeable shortage of staff. But the Ritz kept its rates above 200 ringgit (about $52 U.S.) and was able to pay for low-cost services such as providing the embroidered pillowcases. Most important, the Ritz avoided any damage to its brand equity, something that could have easily occurred if typical Ritz customers arrived at the hotel and found it filled with noisy backpacking tourists or large families, all taking advantage of low prices. The negative spillover onto other Ritz properties could have been significant. The Ritz-Carlton Kuala Lumpur last fall had no more empty rooms than its competitors; in fact, occupancy rates were up to 60% compared with a 50% occupancy rate in 1998. Perhaps most important, monthly gross operating profit on revenue of 2.2 million ringgit is about 400,000 ringgit—a return of about 18%.

Another way companies can avoid a price war is to alert customers to risk—specifically, the risk of poor quality. A senior product manager from the European operation of a large multinational pharmaceutical corporation lamented her recent pricing predicament. Her company's product, a medical diagnostic device, was the market-share leader, but a rival company had recently become aggressive on price

One way companies can avoid a price war is to alert customers to risk—specifically, the risk of poor product quality. A related weapon is to emphasize other negative consequences. Research confirmed that a large segment of customers in this "life and death" industry—doctors and testing laboratories—was quite risk averse and sensitive to variations in a product's performance. So rather than compete on price, the multinational appealed to customers' concerns about performance by emphasizing product enhancements such as improved reliability and greater detail in the information generated by the diagnostic device and by alerting buyers to the negative consequences of incomplete diagnoses. Some sales were lost to lower-priced products from the competitor, but the quality-sensitive segment allowed the multinational to maintain reasonable margins and avoid the negative spiral of a price war.

For Federal Express speed delivery business example, it provides another good example of how a company can appeal to performance sensitivity among customers. FedEx's brand equity exceeds that of virtually any company in the package delivery business. The shipping giant has built an enviable level of consumer recall and recognition through a highly effective advertising campaign. By emphasizing in ads and through other marketing efforts that a customer's package will "absolutely, positively" be there on time, FedEx plays on customers' risk aversion when dealing with time-sensitive documents.

For Coca-Cola or Pepsi and NutraSweet soft drink businesses how to fight prices war example, a related weapon that companies can use to avert or battle a price war is to emphasize other negative consequences. The NutraSweet company employed this strategy when it faced the expiration of its patent. The company feared considerable price pressure from the producers of aspartame, the generic version of NutraSweet. A worst-case scenario would involve one of NutraSweet's major customers, such as Coca-Cola or Pepsi, switching to aspartame. If one of the companies switched, NutraSweet's contingency plan—which it shared with wavering Coke and Pepsi executives in Atlanta and New York—was a week-long advertising blitz that would alert consumers that "the other cola" was the only one that contained NutraSweet. Given the size of the market for carbonated soft drinks, NutraSweet's brand equity in the diet-conscious segment, and the potential short-term loss in market share and profits, this threat had teeth. NutraSweet successfully played one customer against another, emphasizing dire and unpalatable consequences, and thus averted a debilitating price war.

For Japan Sony electronic and North West airline both businesses how to fight prices war example, a final nonprice option involves seeking help, or appealing to contributors to weigh in on the competitive situation. For instance, when Sony entered the market for high-end imaging systems, the leaders in the imaging systems market in Belgium appealed to and received help from the central Belgian government. Not all companies can count on the government to come to their aid, of course. So companies might appeal to customers, vendors, channel partners, independent sales representatives, and other like-minded players if the price war could mean the company's demise. For instance, in the 1990s, Northwest Airlines appealed to its labor unions and received dramatic wage concessions so it could compete on price in a tight air-travel market.

- How to using Selective Pricing Actions to fight prices war for McDonald

Employing complex options such as multiple-part pricing, quantity discounts, time-of-use pricing, bundling, and so on lets price warriors selectively cut rates for only those segments of the population that are under competitive threat. One common—and classic—tactic is to change customers' choices, or reframe the price war in the minds of customers. McDonald's did it successfully when it faced Taco Bell's 59-cent taco strategy in the 1980s. By bundling burgers, fries, and drinks into "value meals," McDonald's reframed the price war from "tacos versus burgers" to "lunch versus lunch." Similarly, smart managers use quantity discounts or loyalty programs to insulate themselves from a price war. They avoid across-the-board price cuts, and they limit price reductions to areas in which they are vulnerable. In this way, managers can localize a price war to a limited theater of operation—and cut down the opportunities for the war to spill into other markets.

For airlines how to selective price action method to fight prices war example, managers can localize a price war to a limited theater of operation—and cut down the opportunities for the war to spill into other markets. Therefore, another selective-pricing tactic might be to modify only certain prices. For instance, Sun Country Airlines, a discount carrier, entered Northwest's Minneapolis–St. Paul hub with 16 planes providing service to 14 cities. Sun Country's round-trip airfare to any location was generally low: Minneapolis to Boston was roughly $308. Rather than engage in a system wide price cut, Northwest retained its existing fare structure with minor modifications. A Minneapolis–Boston round-trip was a relatively low $310 if tickets were purchased seven days in advance—but only for a flight that departed at 7:10 AM and returned at 11:10 AM. Curiously enough, Sun Country's only flight on that route departed Minneapolis at 7 AM and Boston at 11:20 AM. Northwest also employed several other resources, such as travel agents, to fend off Sun Country. Northwest reasoned that Sun Country did not have the infrastructure necessary to engage in an all-out price war and chose to not engage in any preemptive price cutting at times other than the flights directly affected. By targeting only certain fares for discounts, Northwest minimized internal changes but could still counter Sun Country's pricing ploy.

On another selective-pricing front, for diskettes technological companies may use a fighting brand example. In the early 1990s, Kao Corporation entered the diskette market with a low-priced product. Rather than drop its prices, 3M launched a flanking brand of low-priced diskettes called Highland because it knew that a large group of its customers was loyal to the 3M brand. Simply dropping the price on the 3M brand might have diluted 3M's quality image and its profits and may have stimulated further price cuts by Kao.

Because it understood its customers, 3M knew that many different segments of price-sensitive customers existed.

Some people buy cheap diskettes, and some people don't care how much they pay for diskettes. More important, some people think cheap diskettes are probably of poor quality, and they may not buy them if the price is too low—perhaps because they are terrified of losing their data. 3M avoided the trap of charging what the market will bear. It recognized that markets will bear many prices, some better than others. That insight underpins the strategies of many software companies. For instance, marginally different versions of the same voice-recognition software can range in price from $79 to $8,000 depending on who the buyer is.1

That illustration has several instructive elements to it. First, an acute understanding of the competitor's abilities, motives, and mind-set allowed the defending company to react effectively to a price war. Second, the expertise was complemented with a clear understanding of consumer behavior that allowed the company to prevent a price war. Third, the new entrant clearly picked the wrong adversary.

Companies may also opt to cut prices in certain channels. Perhaps the single largest driver of price cuts and resulting price wars is excess capacity. The temptation to revive idle plants by stimulating demand through lower prices is often irresistible. But smart managers consider other options first. For instance, companies in the packaged-goods industry frequently sell off-brand or private-label versions of their national brands at low prices, ensuring that any price wars won't damage the brand equity of the national brands.

For Delta airline how to apply selective price action method to fight prices war example. Similarly, airlines such as Delta are making a dent in reducing their unsold inventory by offering seats to consolidators and auction houses such as

Priceline.com and Cheaptickets.com. The airlines are selling tickets to price-sensitive customers who don't care about flight times, number of stops, or frequent-flyer miles. Because the customer's point of contact is with the consolidator and not with the airline, the airline's image is protected—in much the same way that a nationally branded soup manufacturer protects its image by selling excess capacity under a private label.

the selective price option is a good selling low-priced, functionally equivalent alternatives through unrelated brand names or in foreign markets may still trigger price wars. If consumers recognize that the quality of the private-label product is comparable to that of the branded option, then the price of the branded option will need to drop. In many cases, it is best to leave plant capacity idle, since the attempt to revive it may trigger margin-destroying price competition. In fact, the idle capacity can be used as a weapon; a company then wields the credible threat of being able to flood the market with cheaper products should a competitor start cutting its prices.

Clearly there are times when you must engage in a preemptive strike and start a price war—or respond to a competitor's discount with a matching or deeper price cut of your own. For instance, when a competitor threatens your core business, a retaliatory price cut can be used to signify your intention to fight long and hard. Similarly, when you can identify a large and growing segment of price-sensitive customers, when you have a cost advantage, when your pockets are deeper than competitors' pockets, when you can achieve economies of scale by expanding the market, or when a rival can be neutralized or eliminated because of high barriers to market entry and reentry, then engaging in price competition may be smart.

But there are several long-run implications of competing on price. First, a pattern of price cutting may teach customers to anticipate lower prices; more patient customers will defer their purchases until the next price cut. Second, a price-cutting company develops a reputation for being low-priced, and this reputation may cast doubt on the quality and image of other products under the umbrella brand and on the quality of future products. Third, price cuts have implications for other players in the market, whose self-interest may be harmed by lower prices.

In conclusion, If simple retaliatory price cuts are the chosen means of defense in a price war, implement them quickly and unambiguously so competitors will know that their sales gains will be short-lived as well as if simple retaliatory price cuts are the chosen means of defense in a price war, then implement them quickly and unambiguously so competitors know that their sales gains from a price cut will be short-lived and monetarily unattractive. A slow response may prompt competitors to make additional price cuts in the future.

It's in companies' best interests to reduce price competition because price wars can harm an entire industry. But diplomatic resolutions of price wars are generally impossible because overt diplomacy is a form of price collusion and may attract regulatory oversight. As a result, price leaders often engage in subtle forms of diplomacy that use market forces to discipline renegade companies that threaten industry profits. So "price leadership" is one way to reduce industrywide price competition. Price leaders tend to develop reputations for eschewing price cuts as a way to gain market share and for responding quickly and decisively to price cutting by companies. The price leaders are viewed as credible enforcers of price regimes based on their cost structures, strategic postures, or the personal characteristics of their officers. We do caution, however, that a pattern of disciplinary moves may attract unwelcome regulatory scrutiny; companies should carefully consider whether their attempts at exercising leadership may be interpreted as anticompetitive.

Price wars are a fact of life—whether we're talking about the fast-paced world of "knowledge products," the marketing of Internet appliances, or the staid, traditional business of aluminum castings. If you are not in battle currently, you probably will be fairly soon, so it's never too early to prepare. If you are currently in a price war, understand that you can use several nonprice options to defend yourself . But there's also some buyer's remorse playing out across Wall Street, as remarks by President Donald Trump on Tuesday curtailed some optimism over a China trade deal, and amid talk that investors are too optimistic about U.S. rate cuts. Consumer price inflation numbers may have firmed up those rate-cut prospects a bit. However, several economists and business groups have warned that higher prices from tariffs can hurt American firms and consumers, but the Trump administration continues to defend its policies. Experts predict that some of the first prices to rise will be on computers and computer parts, furniture, and tires. A trade war between the US and China has been heating up for much of this year, and it could have huge impacts on the US economy. President Donald Trump's administration has levied tariffs on a total of $250 billion of imported goods from China. That represents about half of all imports from China. China has retaliated by announcing tariffs on $110 billion of US exports.

- How Tariffs affect the economy

Both Trump's tariffs on China and China's retaliatory tariffs are likely to impact the economy in various ways. At the most basic level, tariffs increase the prices of goods, directly by making imported goods more expensive via the imposed tax, and indirectly by allowing domestic manufacturers who do not have to pay the tariff to charge higher prices. Indeed, that latter effect is the main argument in favor of tariffs: By being able to charge higher prices, domestic producers can theoretically become more profitable and invest more in factories and workers. However, those higher prices can either be passed on to consumers or absorbed by companies buying intermediate products, which can cause economic harm. For Ford Taurus factory Chicago example, Ford has said that tariffs on steel and aluminum imports will likely cost the company $1 billion. For example, Ford says that a separate set of tariffs on steel and aluminum imposed by the Trump administration this spring will likely cost the automaker $1 billion, according to a CBS .

- Consequence of Chinese business against tariffs influence

Higher prices could hit consumers' wallets . US Trading Statistic indicated that the most recent set of tariffs against Chinese imports, which went into effect at the end of September, targeted around $200 billion of goods with a 10% tax scheduled to increase to 25% on January 1, 2019. Unlike earlier rounds of tariffs that mostly targeted materials and intermediate goods, about a quarter of the new tariffs target consumer goods directly, according to an analysis by the Peterson Institute for International Economics.

Those tariffs could have an even more direct impact on Americans' wallets than the earlier round of tariffs, which were mostly against industrial products and intermediate goods. Some of the goods that are likely to be hardest hit by the newer tariffs include computers and computer parts, furniture, and tires. Economists, including Ian Sheperdson of Pantheon Macroeconomics, suggest that consumers could see price increases as a result of tariffs on those goods. "We don't know for sure how quickly importers will raise wholesale prices of the affected items, or how quickly manufacturers of substitutes for Chinese products will lift their prices," Sheperdson wrote in a note to clients. Sheperdson estimated that the newer round of tariffs could add as much as 0.5% to the headline CPI inflation rate. An analysis by the National Taxpayers Union Foundation suggested that the full impact of the 25% tariffs beginning in 2019 would hit Americans harder than the total taxes levied under the Affordable Care Act, better known as Obamacare.

Retailers have also warned that the tariffs could increase prices for consumers and threaten the retail industry.The US Dollar was slammed across the board alongside US equity markets fears of trade wars emerging. It's important for traders to understand the economic significance of tariffs and how they impact economies. To no surprise, US steel and aluminum industry insiders are a fan of the 25% and 10% tariffs that US , respectively. As is often the case with protectionist tariffs, prices for goods using steel and aluminum will rise for the entire economy while these insiders will capture the surplus. In this piece, we'll go in some historical examples of tariffs and their ensuing impacts.

There are three main takeaways why protectionism via

tariffs/limiting free trade is bad:

1) Protectionism always ends up with a bias because it serves to protect "domestic producers in competition with foreign producers." This means protectionist policies like a tariff favor industries in competition with foreign manufacturers over those that are not.

For example, tariffs on imported manufactured goods might be good for domestic US manufacturers, but they'll be bad for anyone else, particularly US agriculture or US service jobs who are not in competition with foreign producers.

2) Protectionism, by its nature, leads to political artifice. Only those in preferred industries – with their goods protected – benefit from tariffs (profit margins are kept intact or boosted), but the costs (retaliatory tariffs from foreign governments or lack of access to cheaper, substitute goods) are shared by society. This makes it a useful tool for politicians to secure political support from say, disaffected workers who have seen their jobs move abroad for cheaper labor. For instance, if the government slaps a tariff on imported steel, the US steel industry will notice the benefit right away while the rest of the country will perceive that they are paying more for any goods with steel in the industrial process. All of the additional surplus created is captured by the producer while the consumer foots the bill. This is bad policy on its own, but it gets substantially worse when unprotected industries plead with Congress for similar favor. The Impact of Tariffs and Trade Wars on the US Economy and the Dollar

3) Protectionism leads directly to political corruption, as politicians become pressured to start protecting every industry. Over time, members of Congress are more or less bribed by corporate executives and titans of industry to

keep the tariffs in place – they protect profit margins, after all.

We benefit from imports because it keeps our cost-of-living down, and preserves our resources. We benefit from exports because we are better than other countries who have higher domestic sources. In other words, I see this trade deficit discussion as a false problem, used by politicians to manipulate voters.

THREE

WHAT STOCK PREDICTION TECHNIQUES ARE THE MOST ACCURATE

If you were to run an autocorrelation filter on virtually any security, you will find price movement is not random. In order to exploit these correlations, you can apply techniques used in speech recognition or other dsp applications. The problem is similar: you want to 'predict' an outcome from noisy signals based on past successful outcomes. Wavelet based denoising in conjunction with hidden markov models, fitted with a global optimizer, are a good place to start.

A large shareholder for example,then working as investment banker, I sat on the other side of the table. With a client, who was either angry (pressuring a fire sale) or afraid that a rating would downgrade him and lower the stock. You could tell what he was going to do. It's also a talent as partner .It's because people are predictable.This specifically counts for the small-cap stocks. The real large quant funds some times really fuck the price of large marketcap stocks. I sometimes wonder who is "fucking who", given I've got colleagues sitting in a variety of firms.

There is no single technique which you can say is most accurate but quantitative techniques are becoming popular nowadays because of their accuracy and scalability. The interesting thing about these techniques are that you can work upon them to improve the techniques easily by analyzing the vast data that comes with them along with the power to combine them with other models.

These techniques involve:

1. Simple mathematical techniques and methods of analyzing .
2. Simple Regression models dealing with autocorrelation etc.
3. Pricing models etc.

These techniques also provides you data quantify your risk which gives you much flexible and creative opportunity to work with your risk management ..

I haven't found an AI programs that are available for stock predictions. But they might be coming soon. In the meantime, I use a quantitative site that is free, Barchart.com | Commodity, Stock, and Currency Quotes, Charts, News & Analysis which shows a broad multi quantitative analysis and I pair that with their 'trading strategies' which show what quant stat actually works for a profitable trade. Finally analysis and peer comparison and whether the stock is over or under priced. Use both, read the news, check their charts (90 day, 1 year, 2 year) to decide if you think it is a decent buy now.

- Recommendation artificial intelligence share price prediction method

We predict future values with technical analysis for wide selection of stocks like Artificial Intelligence Technology Solutions .

What was once thought of as science fiction is now part of our everyday life. Artificial Intelligence and deep learning are topics rarely spoken, artificial intelligence is a sub-field of computer science. The concept of computer system to perform functions using intelligence of a human, such as: visual or audio recognition, computations, decision making, and more. Deep learning is a subfield of machine learning. It is composed of using artificial neural networks consisting of layers to process input data and reach its output result. Such applications are utilized from virtual personal assistants on your phone or computer with Siri, Google Now, or Cortana to fraud detection. And recently, it is being introduced to Amazon first of its kind to offer a shopping experience without the use of cashiers, but instead your phone and visual recognition. By eliminating long lines and reducing labor cost, this could be the future in shopping experience. How did we get here? How is technology continuously finding its use to be applied functionally or in search of answers? Perhaps the biggest question we are asking ourselves is, how can we personally benefit from this?

Investors are constantly in search for strategies and tools to seek consistent or high return on investment given the market's risk. The benefit of utilizing deep learning is its ability to process large amounts of data. It is the challenging for any investor to process such large amounts of data while ignoring the "random noise". The advancement in the use of algorithms and artificial intelligence now accounts for 60-70% of "Buy" and "Sell" orders account of the US equity market volume.

The I Know First self-learning algorithm is used in quantitative trading. This form provides valuable market insight to retail and professional trader alike that is used in conjunction with traditional forms of analysis. Algorithmic traders benefit from this "second opinion" in their decision making process by verifying their own analysis or discovering new market opportunities while still maintaining complete control of their portfolio. These algorithms analyze the structure and the trends in the market, find predictable patterns, and investors trade upon these machine-derived forecasts. This form of trading is very suitable for most investors, retail or professional.

While we cannot speak on every algorithm meant to predict the market, the I Know First market prediction system is based on artificial intelligence (AI), machine learning (ML), as well as utilizes elements of artificial neural networks and genetic algorithms. Machine learning provides an innate acumen to our comprehension of market dynamics and behavior. The algorithm has a built-in general mathematical framework that generates and verifies statistical hypotheses about stock price development. Machine learning tools such as artificial neural networks make this prediction system self-learning, and consistently determined to become more precise. This framework is used to generate initial testing models over a test sample of data. The goal of this phase is to validate the accuracy of the algorithm as well as to fine-tune the fitness function, which represents the actual goal of the algorithm expressed as a mathematical function. When the algorithm finds the global minimum of the fitness function attached to one of the models generated, it fulfills its goal.

Then a learning and prediction cycle is run with the new data included. The algorithm subsequently produces predictions for over 1,400 assets with six time horizons for each. It separates the predictable part from stochastic (random) noise and then creates a model that projects the future trajectory of the given market in the multi-dimensional space of other markets. Thus, I recommend that artificial intelligence (AI) may be the future best tool to help any businesses to predict their share prices whether when they will rise up or fall down in short time to compare other manual share price prediction method.

Intelligent investor

How can we be one intelligent investor? I shall indicate some personal psychological and number analytical methods to explain

how we can avoid investment lose or risk more easily as below:

On personal psychological hand, we need to know when the inflation will come to influence our investment lose. Inflation

have been very much in public's mind in recent years. The shrinkage in the purchasing power of the dollar in the past, and particularly fear (or hope by speculators) of a seriuous further decline in the future, have greatly influenced the share market varies. It is clear that

those with a fixed dollar income will suffer when the cost of living advances, and the same applied to a fixed amount of dollar principal.Holders of stocks, on the other hand, have the possibility that a loss of the dollar's purchasing power may be offset by advances in their dividends and the prices of their shares.

ON the basis of these inflation economic environment changing fact, many financial authorities have concluded that: bonds are an undesirable form of investment and consequently, common stocks are by their very nature more desirable investments than bonds. This is quite a reversal from the earlier
ways when trust investments were restricted by law to high-grade bonds (and a few choice preferrable stocks). How inflation influences
share price change, for example: What would be the implications of such an advance to influence our living when inflation occurs? It would eat up,in higher living costs, about one-half the income now obtainable on good medium -term tax free bonds (or our assumed after -tax equivalet from
high grade corporate bonds). This would be a serious shrinkage, but it should not be exaggerated. It would not mean that the true value, or the purchasing power, of the investor's fortune need be reduced over the years. If the investor spent half his interest income after taxes
he would maintain this buying power intact, even against a 3% annual inflation.

The another personal psychological factor, is that defensive investor psychological investment factor, the basic characteristics of an investment
portfolio are usually determined by the position and characreristics of the owner or owners. At one extreme , we have had savings banks, life insurance companies, and
so-called legal trust funds for our saving methods. A generation ago their investments were limited by law in many states to high grade bonds and in some cases,

high-grade preferred stocks. At the other extreme we have the well -to-do and experienced businessman, who will include any kind of bond or stock in his security list provided he considered it an attractive purchase.

It has been an old and sound principle that those who can't afford to take risks should be content with a relatively low return on their invested funds. From this there has developed the general notion that the rate of return which the investor should aim for is more or less proportionate to the degree of risk he is ready to run. Our view is different. The rate of return sought should be dependent , rather on the amount of intelligent effort the investor is willing and able to bring to bear on his task. The minimum return goes to our passive investor, who wants both safety and freedom from concern. In many cases, there may be less real risk associated with buying a bargain issue offering the chance of a large profit than with a conventional bond purchase yielding about 4.5% . This statement had more truth in it than we ourselves suspected, since in subsequent years even the best long-term bonds lost a substantial part of their market value because of the rise in interest rates.

The another personal psychological factor is that enterprising investor, by definitionm, will devote a fair amount of his attention and efforts towards obtaining a better than run-off-the investment result. In our discussion of general investment policy, we has made some suggestions regarding bond investments that are addresses to the enterprising investor as below:

Tax-free new housinng authority bonds effectively guaranteed by the governments, taxable but high-yield new community bonds , also guaranteed by the governments, and tax -free industrial bonds issued by municipalities, but serviced by lease payments made by strong corporations.

On number analytical methods aspect, it may include industry analysis, because the general prospects of the enterprise carry major weight in the establishment of market price, it is natural for the security analyst to devote a great deal of attention to the economic position of the industry and of the individual company in its industry. Studying these companies' past financial position, they are sometimes productive of valuable insights into important factors that will be operative in the future and are insufficiently appreciated by the current market. Where a conclusion of that kind can be drawn with a degree of confidence, it affords a sound basis for investment decisions.

Our own observation, however leads us to minimum somewhat the practical value of most of the industry studies that are made available to investors. The material developed is ordinarily of a kind with which the public is already fairly familiar and that has already considerable influence on market quotations. Rarely does one find a brokerage-house study that points out, with a popular industry is heading for a fall or that an unpopular one is due to prosper. For example, Wall street's view of the longer future is fallible and this necessarily applies to that importanr part of its investigations which is directed towards the forecasting of the course of profits in various industries.

ON predicting growth stock investing style hand, growth companies have above average-growth rates of sales and/ or earnings. Growth investors are willing to pay high multiples of earnings for companies with high growth rates, which explains why growth stocks generally have high P/E multiples. For Starbucks office business case

example, it has a high P/E multiple of 28 , and the multiple could expand as the company grows at its expected rate. If growth stocks do not sustain their high growth rates, their stock prices are severely punished, as we saw with momentum stock Chipotle Mexican Grill. For Apple computer share example, it is a good example of a growth stock. It has high sustained growth from sales
of its iPad, iPhone, and iPod products, which are dominant in tehir respective markets, and they stil have the ability to increase their market shares. Apple computer has been more
innovative than its competitiors, which also underscores its strong management. In addition, Apple paid a 1.57 percent dividend in Sept. 2012, which somewhat a potential fall in the stock price as a result of future disappointing earnings or reduced future estimates of growth. Moreover, in the past record, Apple's stock price for the year from Sept, 2011 to Aug, 2012 shows a BETTER chart pattern than that of Chipotle Mexican Grill , illustrating the risk when momentum stocks fall out of favor. From a value investor's vire, there is more value in Apple stock than in Chipotle Mexican Grill in the futuer. Apple has a strong balance asset in that it has $20 billion in cash and has no long -term debt. Its liquidity is good,
meaning it can easily convert its current assets into cash to pay off its current liabilities (bills) as they come due. Yet despite paying a 1.57 percent dividend yield, it is still very much a growth stock. The company trades at roughly eight times book value and its P/E multiple is around sixteen times its earnings. As long as Apple delivers on its growth in sales and
earnings, its stock price will continue to rise. The downside to growth stocks is that should companies fail to grow as

rapidly as expected, their stock prices will be punished more severely than value stocks because expectations for growrh stocks are much greater than those for value stocks. So, any investors can seek any companies' past financial performance and
stock price to predict their stock price whether it can rises up or falles down in the short times, e.g. one to three months. Because it will have unpredictable environment factors can influence any companies stock sale number effort in long term. So, I mean that predicting long time stock price changes whether either is increasing or decreasing, it is more difficult to compare to predict its' stock price changes in short time.

Finally, any investors can attempt to follow these rewards and risks to stocks' past record to judge whether the company's stock price will rises up or falls down
in order to decide investment: ON rewards aspect, is the stock price less than two-thirds of the book value of the stock? Is the stock price less than two -thirds of the net
current asset value per share (current assets minus total debt)? On the risks aspect, is the debt-t-o-equity ratio less than one? The total debt of the company should be less than total equity? Is the current ratio equal to rwo or more? The total current assets divided by the total current liabilities should equal two or more? Is the total debt less than twice the net current assets? Is the 10 year average EPS (earning per share) growth rate greater than 7 % ? Were there no more than two years our of the past 10 with earnings declines of greater than 5 %? Moreover, any investors can also analyze how the company's financial performance changed from these information:
Whether the company seeks long term captial appreciation through the growth of the fund's value over a period of time

or short term captial appreciation objective? To seek current income through investments that generate dividends and to preserve investors' principal. What are the companies' strategies, e.g. the manager of a stock fund might buy growth or value stocks of companies with a particular size capitalization (small-cap, medium-cap, large-cap stocks). Thusm a value investor looking for a large -cap value fund can comapre the different funds offering these types of securities. Estimating the company's overall performance fund from its' past total return and expenses in order to predict its profit or loss in current year and stock price can be influenced to rise up or fall down in possible.

Thus, in any country stock market, one intelligent investor can attempt to apply personal psychological and number analytical methods to predict any stock price changes more accurately to compare
other professionals or friends or families those investing opinions.

FOUR

HOW TO PREDICT SHARE PRICE

What does stock market prediction mean ? Stock market prediction is the act of trying to determine the future value of a company stock or other financial instrument traded on an exchange. The successful prediction of a stock's future price could yield significant profit. The efficient-market hypothesis suggests that stock prices reflect all currently available information and any price changes that are not based on newly revealed information thus are inherently unpredictable. Others disagree and those with this viewpoint possess myriad methods and technologies which purportedly allow them to gain future price information.

Intrinsic value (true value) is the perceived or calculated value of a company, including tangible and intangible factors, using fundamental analysis. It's also frequently called fundamental value. It is used for comparison with the company's market value and finding out whether the company is undervalued on the stock market or not. When calculating it, the investor looks at both the qualitative and quantitative aspects of the business. It is ordinarily calculated by summing the discounted future income generated by the asset to obtain the present value.

Prediction methodologies fall into three broad categories which can (and often do) overlap. They are fundamental analysis, technical analysis (charting) and technological methods as below:

Fundamental analysis

Fundamental Analysts are concerned with the company that underlies the stock itself. They evaluate a company's past performance as well as the credibility of its accounts. Many performance ratios are created that aid the fundamental analyst with assessing the validity of a stock, such as the P/E ratio. Warren Buffett is perhaps the most famous of all Fundamental Analysts.

What fundamental analysis in stock market is trying to achieve, is finding out the true value of a stock, which then can be compared with the value it is being traded with on stock markets and therefore finding out whether the stock on the market is undervalued or not. Finding out the true value can be done by various methods with basically the same principle. The principle being that a company is worth all of its future profits added together. These future profits also have to be discounted to their present value. This principle goes along well with the theory that a business is all about profits and nothing else. Contrary to technical analysis, fundamental analysis is thought of more as a long-term strategy.

Fundamental analysis is built on the belief that human society needs capital to make progress and if a company operates well, it should be rewarded with additional capital and result in a surge in stock price. Fundamental analysis is widely used by fund managers as it is the most reasonable, objective and made from publicly available information

like financial statement analysis.
Another meaning of fundamental analysis is beyond bottom-up company analysis, it refers to top-down analysis from first analyzing the global economy, followed by country analysis and then sector analysis, and finally the company level analysis.

Technical analysis

Technical analysts or chartists are not concerned with any of the company's fundamentals. They seek to determine the future price of a stock based solely on the trends of the past price (a form of time series analysis). Numerous patterns are employed such as the head and shoulders or cup and saucer. Alongside the patterns, techniques are used such as the exponential moving average (EMA), oscillators, support and resistance levels or momentum and volume indicators. Candle stick patterns, believed to have been first developed by Japanese rice merchants, are nowadays widely used by technical analysts. Technical analysis is rather used for short-term strategies, than the long-term ones. And therefore, it is far more prevalent in commodities and forex markets where traders focus on short-term price movements. There are some basic assumptions used in this analysis, first being that everything significant about a company is already priced into the stock, other being that the price moves in trends and lastly that history (of prices) tends to repeat itself which is mainly because of the market psychology.

Machine learning

With the advent of the digital computer, stock market prediction has since moved into the technological realm. The most prominent technique involves the use of artificial neural networks (ANNs) and Genetic Algorithms(GA). Scholars found bacterial chemotaxis optimization method may perform better than GA.[1] ANNs can be thought of as mathematical function approximators. The most common form of ANN in use for stock market prediction is the feed forward network utilizing the backward propagation of errors algorithm to update the network weights. These networks are commonly referred to as Backpropagation networks. For stock prediction with ANNs, there are usually two approaches taken for forecasting different time horizons: independent and joint. The independent approach employs a single ANN for each time horizon, for example, 1-day, 2-day, or 5-day. The advantage of this approach is that network forecasting error for one horizon won't impact the error for another horizon—since each time horizon is typically a unique problem. The joint approach, however, incorporates multiple time horizons together so that they are determined simultaneously. In this approach, forecasting error for one time horizon may share its error with that of another horizon, which can decrease performance. There are also more parameters required for a joint model, which increases the risk of overfitting. Of late, the majority of academic research groups studying ANNs for stock forecasting seem to be using an ensemble of independent ANNs methods more frequently, with greater success. An ensemble of ANNs would use low price and time lags to predict future lows, while another network would use lagged highs to predict future highs. The predicted low and high predictions are then used to form stop prices for buying or selling. Outputs from the individual "low" and "high" networks can also be input into a final network that would also incorporate volume, intermarket data or statistical summaries of prices, leading to a final ensemble output that would trigger buying, selling, or market directional change. A major finding with

ANNs and stock prediction is that a classification approach (vs. function approximation) using outputs in the form of buy(y=+1) and sell(y=-1) results in better predictive reliability than a quantitative output such as low or high price. Since NNs require training and can have a large parameter space; it is useful to optimize the network for optimal predictive ability.

Can share buyer or investor predict the company's share price whether when it will rise or fall ? If any shareholder can predict any firm's share price whether it will rise or fall in the month. Then, he will not lose , even earn share profit more easily. For example, when the shareholder had bought 100 share and every share $1 for the company shares. If he can predict the firm 's shares will rise 50% next month. Although, the firm's share price is falling in this month. Because he predicts the firm's share price will rise 50% next month. So, he won't be influenced to sell his all 100 shares for the firm. He will sell all his shares to earn profit next month. The question is how he can predict the firm's share price when it will rise. I have some recommedation as below:

Predict Market Performance

There are two prices that are critical for any investor to know: the current price of the investment he or she owns or plans to own and its future selling price. Despite this, investors are constantly reviewing past pricing history and using it to influence their future investment decisions. Some investors won't buy a stock or index that has risen too sharply, because they assume it's due for a correction, while other investors avoid a falling stock because they fear it will continue to deteriorate. Does academic evidence support these types of predictions, based on recent pricing? In this article, we'll look at four different views of the market and learn more about the associated academic research that supports each view. The conclusions will help you better understand how the market functions and perhaps eliminate some of your own biases.

This widely quoted piece of stock market wisdom warns investors not to get in the way of market trends. The assumption is that the best bet about market movements is that they will continue in the same direction. This concept has its roots in behavioral finance. With so many stocks to choose from, why would investors keep their money in a stock that's falling, as opposed to one that's climbing? It's classic fear and greed. Studies have found that mutual fund inflows are positively correlated with market returns. Momentum plays a part in the decision to invest and when more people invest, the market goes up, encouraging even more people to buy. It's a positive feedback loop.

Mean Reversion

Experienced investors, who have seen many market ups and downs, often take the view that the market will even out, over time. Historically, high market prices often discourage these investors from investing, while historically low prices may represent an opportunity. The tendency of a variable, such as a stock price, to converge on an average value over time is called mean reversion. The phenomenon has been found in several economic indicators, which are useful to know, including exchange rates, gross domestic product (GDP) growth, interest rates, and unemployment. A mean reversion may also be responsible for business cycles.

The tendency of a variable, such as a stock price, to converge on an average value over time is called mean reversion. The phenomenon has been found in several economic indicators, which are useful to know, including exchange rates, gross domestic product (GDP) growth, interest rates, and unemployment. A mean reversion may also be responsible for business cycles.e jury is still out about whether stock prices revert to the mean. Some studies show mean reversion in some data sets over some periods, but many others do not. For example, in 2000, Ronald Balvers, Yangru Wu and Erik Gilliland found some evidence of mean reversion over long investment horizons, in the relative stock index prices of 18 countries. However, even they weren't completely convinced, as they wrote in their study, "A serious obstacle in detecting mean reversion is the absence of reliable long-term series, especially because mean-reversion, if it exists, is thought to be slow and can only be picked up over long horizons."

Martingales

Another possibility is that past returns just don't matter. In 1965, Paul Samuelson studied market returns and found that past pricing trends had no effect on future prices and reasoned that in an efficient market, there should be no such effect. His conclusion was that market prices are martingales.

A martingale is a mathematical series in which the best prediction for the next number is the current number. The concept is used in probability theory, to estimate the results of random motion. For example, suppose that you have $50 and bet it all on a coin toss. How much money will you have after the toss? You may have $100 or you may have $0 after the toss, but statistically, the best prediction is $50 -- your original starting position. The prediction of your fortunes after the toss is a martingale.

In stock option pricing, stock market returns could be assumed to be martingales. According to this theory, the valuation of the option does not depend on the past pricing trend, or on any estimate of future price trends. The current price and the estimated volatility are the only stock-specific inputs.

A martingale in which the next number is more likely to be higher is known as a sub-martingale. In popular literature, this motion is known as a random walk with upward drift. This description is consistent with more than 80 years of stock market pricing history. Despite many short-term reversals, the overall trend has been consistently higher.

If stock returns are essentially random, the best prediction for tomorrow's market price is simply today's price, plus a very small increase. Rather than focusing on past trends and looking for possible momentum or mean reversion, investors should instead concentrate on managing the risk inherent in their volatile investments.

The Search for Value

Value investors purchase stock cheaply and expect to be rewarded later. Their hope is that an inefficient market has underpriced the stock, but that the price will adjust over time. The question is: Does this happen, and why would an inefficient market make this adjustment?

Research suggests this mispricing and readjustment consistently happens, although it presents very little evidence for why it happens. In 1964, Gene Fama and Ken French studied decades of stock market history and developed the three-factor model to explain stock market prices. The most significant factor in explaining future price returns was valuation as measured by the price-to-book ratio (P/B). Stocks with low price-to-book ratios delivered significantly better returns than other stocks.

Valuation ratios tend to move in the same direction and in 1977, Sanjoy Basu found similar results for stocks with low price-earnings (P/E) ratios. Since then, the same effect has been found in many other studies across dozens of markets. However, studies have not explained why the market is consistently mispricing these "value" stocks and then adjusting later. The only conclusion that could be drawn is that these stocks have extra risk, for which investors demand additional compensation for taking extra risk. Price is the driver of the valuation ratios, therefore, the findings do support the idea of a mean-reverting stock market. As prices climb, the valuation ratios get higher and, as a result, future predicted returns are lower. However, the market P/E ratio has fluctuated widely over time and has never been a consistent buy or sell signal.

The Bottom Line

Even after decades of study by the brightest minds in finance, there are no solid answers. The only conclusion that can be drawn is that there may be some momentum effects, in the short term and a weak mean-reversion effect, in the long term.The current price is a key component of valuation ratios such as P/B and P/E, that have been shown to have some predictive power on the future returns of a stock. However, these ratios should not be viewed as specific buy and sell signals, but as factors that have been shown to play a role in increasing or reducing the expected long-term return.

All of above four kinds of calculation methods can be suitable to attempt to predict any share price variation whether it will rise or fall next month. The another method is that studying the firm's past financial performance. It is one good analysis method to attempt to predict its future share price variation from its past five to ten years performance.

Whether you are looking for good investments or are into

stock trading, stock prediction or forecast plays the most crucial role in determining where to put in the money or which stock to be acquired or sold. Market trends often reflect the mood of the market and not essentially the status of a company or the true value of the stocks. It is often that stock prices soar based on external factors and it is not uncommon to find stock traders and investors to base their decisions on current affairs and market trends while trying to forecast the stock of any specific company. Stocks are volatile primarily owing to these reasons since external factors and popular beliefs are almost always based on no solid foundation. Consequentially, the stock prediction goes awry. The two stock forecasting methods any investor or stock trader must use are the Fundamental Research and Stock Forecast Algorithms.

Fundamental Research is a mandatory method for any investor. The method involves meticulous studying of a company's financial health, the value of assets, debts, cash, revenues, expenses, profitability and plans of development. Fundamental Research is a well rounded stock prediction method for all the data that actually matters are taken into consideration while determining the true value of a stock A company may generate healthy revenue but owing to huge expenses, they may not be highly profitable. It is common for a well performing company to sit on a pile of cash and not use it wisely in other investment or diversification avenues. Having all these statistics can be very handy for any investor. Once you have all this information, it is easy to determine if the value of a stock is overhyped or below par. Thus, it is easier to forecast the future of a stock and determine whether to acquire a stock or to sell one. Fundamental Research also helps an investor since it offers insights to dividends the company has been paying over the years and you can have some statistical stock prediction and not just volatility.

But knowing fundamentals is not enough. It is common for stocks to move in waves. Stocks always fluctuate between "oversold" and "overbought" conditions. These terms describe the changing demand or popularity, and are relative to the time frame and to other investment venues. When gold becomes popular, lots of investors get caught in the "Gold Rush" and forget the stock fundamentals and sell stocks to buy gold. They forget that gold does not make anything and just sits there. It's just a trophy, a protection against inflation at best. This is just one example of how different markets interact. Thus knowing the stock fundamentals is not enough. One can buy a good stock at the wrong time and lose money. Sure, eventually it should pay off, but meanwhile, you are in a deficit. Thus you have to be able to predict where the stock is heading.

Stock Forecast Algorithms are aimed at making the best use of the right time, right price and the right quantity of stocks that must be traded. The Algorithm in place helps a trader to forecast the time at which the price would be the most favorable to either buy or sell a stock. The system predicts absolutely on numbers and has not even remotely affected by popular emotions.

Finally, one should not get caught up in the daily trading, and miss out on global trends. This has been a decade of raise of China as the world's strongest growing economy, the fall of Europe and its Euro, and the crisis in the USA. The excesses of fiscal policy, the foolish flight of the US industry into the cheap labor countries, and the expensive wars have ravaged the economy and weakened the US dollar. But all this is behind us, and it seems that these trends have come to the stall. Will they reverse their course? All this requires us to look at the different time ranges of predictions, not only the next week predictions, but also the longer term forecasts. Don't assume that you will be lucky to get out in time. Downward corrections can come rather quickly and be sharper than the upward moves.

What are some mathematical methods which are used to predict stock price movement?

Can mathematical models beat markets? Science is about empirical fact. There is no question that optimistic people think they can beat the market, but they don't do it consistently with mathematical models. No model can consistently predict the future. It can't possibly be.

So what can math predict?

What you can do is predict the risk of a given event. The risk just means the chance that something bad will happen, for example. That you can do with increasing accuracy because we have more and more data. It's like insurance companies: they cannot tell you when you are going to die, but they can predict the risk that you will die given the right information. You can do the same thing with stocks. If you lose less, you get ahead of those who lose more.

Why do economists and "quants"—those who use quantitative analysis to make financial trades—have such faith in their mathematical models then?

If they're just to reduce risk, then they're very valuable. If you're worried, for example, about the segment of the Chinese economy that deals with steel, you make a model of what that whole market is all about and then you see if we did this what would likely happen. They're right some of the time. It's better than nothing. But when they have excessive faith in these models, it's not justified. Math starts with assumptions; the real world does not work that way. Economics, which calls itself a science, too often doesn't start with looking at empirical facts in any great detail. Fifteen years ago even the idea of looking at huge amounts of data did not exist. With a limited amount of data, the chance of a rare event is very low, which gave some economists a false sense of security that long-tail events did not exist.

Why do you argue that financial markets are ruled not by Gaussian functions but by power laws—relations in which the frequency of one event varies as a power of some attribute of that event and are generally more L-shape than bell shape? For anything that is random and fluctuating, like a financial market, a Gaussian function is a wonderful way to make a histogram of the outcome.

The catch is: in a financial market, everything is correlated. The proof of that is that if the stock market were Gaussian, then you'd never have a flash crash. A Gaussian crash would be an event that goes out to maybe five standard deviations [that is, a rarity on par with one part in two million]. In markets, this is simply not true. There are events that are 100 standard deviations. Every economist knows for sure that these rare events occur and cannot be described by a Gaussian function. The question is: What are you going to do about it?

Power math laws are simply way more accurate. If you don't know the risk, you are not going to make the right decision, and the economy is at risk from these big fluctuations. It's no surprise when they come. The only reason you have to wait awhile is because they are rare. Knowing that they will happen forces anyone prudent to have a plan for what to do if it happens. The idea that it would be a power law that describes all the events, the tails and the middle is really a major contribution. It allows one to quantify risk. You can read off a plot of the law the numerical chance for a downturn of any given size. It's very small for something that is 100 standard deviations out but not so small for something that is 10 standard deviations out. In fact, the S&P 500 fluctuations—which if they were Gaussian, would pretty much be constrained to plus or minus five standard deviations—you find, in a 10-year period, the number of events that exceed five standard deviations is not just one, it's 64. And the number that exceeds 10 standard deviations is eight, and there was one event that exceeded 20 standard deviations. It looks like a power law, and that's what it is demonstrated to be when every trade of every stock is analyzed.

Does this understanding of financial markets suggest anything about how to invest, like when to buy or sell? It can't predict the future. The key thing is that it tells you not to listen to those who tell you now is the time to buy or sell if their advice is based on something wrong, as it sometimes is.

Is this all a result of the interlinked global financial system?I believe so. The finances of every country are interlinked to the finances of every other country and, because they are interlinked, if one key players goes down then the other players know things aren't going to be as good. A useful analogy is coupled networks, which are far more susceptible to a cascade of failures than uncoupled networks.

Can anything predict the market? Let me tell you a story: two to the power of 10 is 1,024. One way to predict the market is to call up 1,024 trading places and tell half of them by week's end the market will be up and the other half that the market will be down. At the end of the week, forget about the half that knows you were wrong. Keep doing that for 10 weeks and, at the end, you will have called the market correctly for one person who will think you are a genius. The economy is a very complex system—like the weather—that we understand bits of. You sure as heck can't decide on a Monday whether the weather will be nice on the coming weekend. No one can predict where the market will be at the end of the week.

For math prediction to share price variation example:

The best model we have to predict stock price movements is the Random Walk model.

$R(t+1) = R(t) + e$

It basically states that returns on a stock tomorrow can be calculated using the return today plus an error term. An error term is the deviation of reality from your model that cannot be calculated by your model. If it was possible to be calculated, it should have been integrated into your model. This answer tells you nothing except the fact that stock prices are a result of multiple variables, some of which cannot be quantified (sentiment premiums).

Unfortunately, the accuracy of any mathematical model to predict the stock price movement is lower. However, you can use a concept of statistical arbitrage where you predict the relative value of the stock price compared to another stock price. For instance, you can trade on the difference (spread) between prices of two stocks which are cointegrated and use a mathematical model or historical data to predict if the spread is high or low and trade accordingly. An example of a portfolio of possibly cointegrated stocks is the spread between gold ETF (GLD) and gold miners ETF (GDX). The new series "GLD - GDX" forms a stationary portfolio and gives us an opportunity to create a mean-reverting strategy: buy when the spread is low and sell when the spread is high.

Hence, it is very difficult to predict a stock price in the

future with more than 10% certainty. Anything above that confidence interval is overestimation of your abilities and pure luck. t seems that investors can attempt to apply math method to predict share price when changes, although it may have wrong chance to estimate the price changes to rise or fall price absolutely. However, it can conclude the minimum price estimation in error to compare the share investor himself/herself personal judgement to the share price.

FIVE

EVALUATION TO SHARE PRICE CHANGE FACTORS

Stock prices are determined in the marketplace, where seller supply meets buyer demand. But have you ever wondered about what drives the stock market—that is, what factors affect a stock's price? Unfortunately, there is no clean equation that tells us exactly how a stock price will behave. That said, we do know a few things about the forces that move a stock up or down. These forces fall into three categories: fundamental factors, technical factors, and market sentiment.

•Stock prices are driven by a variety of factors, but ultimately the price at any given moment is due to the supply and demand at that point in time in the market.

•Fundamental factors drive stock prices based on a company's earnings and profitability from producing and selling goods and services.

·Technical factors relate to a stock's price history in the market pertaining to chart patterns, momentum, and behavioral factors of traders and investors.

Fundamental Factors

In an efficient market, stock prices would be determined primarily by fundamentals, which, at the basic level, refer to a combination of two things:

1.An earnings base, such as earnings per share (EPS)
2.A valuation multiple, such as a P/E ratio

An owner of common stock has a claim on earnings, and earnings per share (EPS) is the owner's return on his or her investment. When you buy a stock, you are purchasing a proportional share of an entire future stream of earnings. That's the reason for the valuation multiple: It is the price you are willing to pay for the future stream of earnings.

What Moves Stock Prices?

Part of these earnings may be distributed as dividends, while the remainder will be retained by the company (on your behalf) for reinvestment. We can think of the future earnings stream as a function of both the current level of earnings and the expected growth in this earnings base.

valuation multiple (P/E), or the stock price as some multiple of EPS, is a way of representing the discounted present value of the anticipated future earnings stream.

The Earnings Base

Although we are using EPS, an accounting measure, to illustrate the concept of earnings base, there are other measures of earnings power. Many argue that cash-flow-based measures are superior. For example, free cash flow per share is used as an alternative measure of earnings power.

The way earnings power is measured may also depend on

the type of company being analyzed. Many industries have their own tailored metrics. Real estate investment trusts (REITs), for example, use a special measure of earnings power called funds from operations (FFO). Relatively mature companies are often measured by dividends per share, which represents what the shareholder actually receives.

The Valuation Multiple

The valuation multiple expresses expectations about the future. As we already explained, it is fundamentally based on the discounted present value of the future earnings stream. Therefore, the two key factors here are:

1.The expected growth in the earnings base

2.The discount rate, which is used to calculate the present value of the future stream of earnings

A higher growth rate will earn the stock a higher multiple, but a higher discount rate will earn a lower multiple.What determines the discount rate? First, it is a function of perceived risk. A riskier stock earns a higher discount rate, which, in turn, earns a lower multiple. Second, it is a function of inflation (or interest rates, arguably). Higher inflation earns a higher discount rate, which earns a lower multiple (meaning the future earnings are going to be worth less in inflationary environments).

In summary, the key fundamental factors are:

·The level of the earnings base (represented by measures such as EPS, cash flow per share, dividends per share)

·The expected growth in the earnings base

·The discount rate, which is itself a function of inflation

·The perceived risk of the stock

Technical Factors

Things would be easier if only fundamental factors set stock prices. Technical factors are the mix of external conditions that alter the supply of and demand for a company's stock. Some of these indirectly affect fundamentals. For example, economic growth indirectly contributes to earnings growth.

Technical factors include the following:

Inflation factor influences shares prices variable

We mentioned it earlier as an input into the valuation multiple, but inflation is a huge driver from a technical perspective as well. Historically, low inflation has had a strong inverse correlation with valuations (low inflation drives high multiples and high inflation drives low multiples). Deflation, on the other hand, is generally bad for stocks because it signifies a loss in pricing power for companies.

Economic Strength of Market and Peers factor influences shares prices variable

Company stocks tend to track with the market and with their sector or industry peers. Some prominent investment firms argue that the combination of overall market and sector movements—as opposed to a company's individual performance—determines a majority of a stock's movement. (Research has suggested the economic/market factors account for 90 percent of it.) For example, a suddenly negative outlook for one retail stock often hurts other retail stocks as "guilt by association" drags down demand for the whole sector.

Substitutes factor influences shares prices variable

Companies compete for investment dollars with other asset classes on a global stage. These include corporate bonds, government bonds, commodities, real estate, and foreign equities. The relationship between demand for U.S. equities and their substitutes is hard to figure, but it plays an important role.

Incidental Transactions factor influences shares prices variable

Incidental transactions are purchases or sales of a stock that are motivated by something other than belief in the intrinsic value of the stock. These transactions include executive insider transactions, which are often pre-scheduled or driven by portfolio objectives. Another example is an institution buying or shorting a stock to hedge some other investment. Although these transactions may not represent official "votes cast" for or against the stock, they do impact supply and demand and, therefore, can move the price.

Demographics factor influences shares prices variable

Some important research has been done about the demographics of investors. Much of it concerns these two dynamics:

1.Middle-aged investors, peak earners who tend to invest in the stock market

2.Older investors, who tend to pull out of the market in order to meet the demands of retirement

The hypothesis is that the greater the proportion of middle-aged investors among the investing population, the greater the demand for equities and the higher the valuation multiples.

Trends changing factor influences shares prices variable

Often a stock simply moves according to a short-term trend. On the one hand, a stock that is moving up can gather momentum, as "success breeds success" and popularity buoys the stock higher. On the other hand, a stock sometimes behaves the opposite way in a trend and does what is called reverting to the mean. Unfortunately, because trends cut both ways and are more obvious in hindsight, knowing that stocks are "trendy" does not help us predict the future.

Liquidity factor influences shares prices variable

Liquidity is an important and sometimes under-appreciated factor. It refers to how much interest from investors a specific stock attracts. Wal-Mart's stock, for example, is highly liquid and therefore highly responsive to material news; the average small-cap company is less so. Trading volume is not only a proxy for liquidity, but it is also a function of corporate communications (that is, the degree to which the company is getting attention from the investor community). Large-cap stocks have high liquidity—they are well followed and heavily transacted. Many small-cap stocks suffer from an almost permanent "liquidity discount" because they simply are not on investors' radar screens.

News information delivering factor influences shares prices variable

While it is hard to quantify the impact of news or unexpected developments inside a company, industry or the global economy, you can't argue that it does influence investor sentiment. The political situation, negotiations between countries or companies, product breakthroughs, mergers and acquisitions and other unforeseen events can impact stocks and the stock market. Since securities trading happens across the world and markets and economies are interconnected, news in one country can impact investors in another, almost instantly.

Market Sentiment factor influences shares prices variable

Market sentiment refers to the psychology of market

participants, individually and collectively. This is perhaps the most vexing category. Market sentiment is often subjective, biased, and obstinate. For example, you can make a solid judgment about a stock's future growth prospects, and the future may even confirm your projections, but in the meantime, the market may myopically dwell on a single piece of news that keeps the stock artificially high or low. And you can sometimes wait a long time in the hope that other investors will notice the fundamentals.

Market sentiment is being explored by the relatively new field of behavioral finance. It starts with the assumption that markets are apparently not efficient much of the time, and this inefficiency can be explained by psychology and other social science disciplines. The idea of applying social science to finance was fully legitimized when Daniel Kahneman, PhD, a psychologist, won the 2002 Nobel Memorial Prize in Economic Sciences (the first psychologist to do so). Many of the ideas in behavioral finance confirm observable suspicions: that investors tend to overemphasize data that come easily to mind; that many investors react with greater pain to losses than with pleasure to equivalent gains; and that investors tend to persist in a mistake.

Some investors claim to be able to capitalize on the theory of behavioral finance. For the majority, however, the field is new enough to serve as the "catch-all" category, where everything we cannot explain is deposited.

The Bottom Line factor influences shares prices variable Different types of investors depend on different factors. Short-term investors and traders tend to incorporate and may even prioritize technical factors. Long-term investors prioritize fundamentals and recognize that technical factors play an important role. Investors who believe strongly in fundamentals can reconcile themselves to technical forces with the following popular argument: technical factors and market sentiment often overwhelm the short run, but fundamentals will set the stock price in the long-run. In the meantime, we can expect more exciting developments in the area of behavioral finance, especially since traditional financial theories cannot seem to explain everything that happens in the market.

- Trading Basics- Factors that Influence Share Prices

The Market Place

The marketplace determines share prices. While seller supply and buyer demand meet in the market, there is no perfect equation that lets investors know exactly how share prices will behave. However, there a number of factors that can move stocks up and down.

Demand and Supply

It means that how many shares , the company issue and how many number , the shareholders choose to buy the firm's shares in the month.Demand and supply in the market affect the prices of shares. When demand for shares exceeds supply, which means the buyers are more than sellers, the prices increase. When demand is less than supply, meaning that buyers are less than sellers, the prices decrease.

Interest Rates

In case of lower interest rates, demand for funds is higher and the subsequent demand for shares rises. On the other hand, high interest lowers the demand for funds and the demand for shares is lower.

Investors

Market players have an impact on share prices. With more bulls than bears, the prices increase. With more bears than bulls, share prices decline.

Dividends

Dividends indicate the movement of share prices. When companies make dividend announcements, the share prices of such companies are likely to increase. It is important to note that if the dividend rate announced is lower than the investors' expectations, share prices decline while if they are up to more than expected, share prices increase.

Management

Management profile has a significant effect on company success and stock prices. If management consists of experienced professionals with a proven track record, share prices are likely to be higher. If the management that takes over a company lacks integrity, share prices tend to fall.

Economy

Fluctuations in the economy feature what are commonly referred to as booms and depressions. Under favorable conditions share prices are at their peak and their lowest point is experienced during depressions. Share prices gradually rise during recovery and fall during recessions. Click here for live Lloyds share price.

Political Climate

Political factors that range from relations with other nations to government policies can affect share prices.

Short-Term and Long-Term Investors

Different investors rely on different factors. A short-term trader or investor is likely to prioritize and incorporate technical factors such as inflation, trends and demographics. Long-term investors focus on fundamentals like earning power and acknowledge the crucial role that technical factors play. Investors who prioritize fundamentals can integrate technical factors.

It is widely believed that market sentiment and technical

factors are overwhelming on a short-term basis but fundamentals ultimately set share prices in the long run. Since conventional theories are not sufficient for explaining all the things that go on in the market, behavioral finance or market sentiment will always be a keen area of interest.

Industrial relations

In case there is good relationship between the workers and the management of a company, the productivity would be high leading to better profits. Therefore share prices would be higher. In case of companies where industrial relations are poor and strikes and lockouts occur regularly, performance of the company would be poor. Therefore share prices would fall.

Stability of government

When there is a stable government, businessmen feel confident to invest in new businesses and expand existing businesses. Production, sales and profits are higher and consequently share prices would increase. In case of instability in the government, new investments do not take place. Demand, production and profits are lower and share prices fall.

General market sentiments

It is generally said that sentiments move the markets. If there is optimism among market players, more buying would take place leading to increase in share prices. In case market players are pessimistic, then more selling would take place pushing down share prices.

Actions of institutional investors

Share prices are influenced by Institutional investors such as mutual funds, investment trusts, pension funds etc. They have large amount of funds at their disposal. When they start buying, share prices would increase and when they sell, share prices decline

Level of foreign investment

In recent times, the level of foreign institutional investors (FII's) have played a significant role in influencing share prices. If the level of foreign investment in the market increases (more buying of shares), then the share prices increase. If the level of foreign investment decreases of if FII's sell their investments, then the markets fall.

Returns offered by other markets

If the Indian markets offer high returns, institutional investors (especially FII's) would invest in Indian markets. Demand for shares would increase and prices rise. In case returns offered by markets in other countries are attractive, then institutional investors would sell their securities in order to invest in those markets. In such cases, shares would be sold in large quantities lowering prices.

Availability of credit

In case credit is available without much restriction, then investors would borrow to invest in the markets. Demand for shares would be more and therefore prices rise. In case credit is restricted, then the level of borrowing would be less and demand for shares would also be lower.

Effective regulation

If the stock market is run in a transparent manner with effective regulation then the investors would feel confident to invest. Therefore more buying would take place and share prices increase. But when regulation is ineffective and if scams occur (Harshad Mehta scam, MS Shoes scam, CRB scam, Ketan Parekh scam and the recent IPO scam) investors would lose confidence. They would panic and sell their shares. So prices would fall.

Considerations

·Stock prices change for various reasons. While some

people believe that it is impossible to predict the changes, others think that observing past price movements and charts can determine when you should buy and sell.

·Stocks are volatile, which means that prices can rapidly change.

·Fundamentally, demand and supply in the market influence share price.

·Comparing the share prices of two different companies is not conclusive when determining the value of a company.

● What factors increase earnings per share?

Earnings per Share = (Revenue - Cost) / Share Count

So there's really 3 key factors that increase EPS:

1.Revenue Increase: A higher revenue means more dollar flowing down to earnings. Revenue is a function of price and volume. So Revenue can increase if:

a.Volume of products sold increases; and/or

b.Average price of products sold increases

2.Cost Decrease: A lower cost means a greater portion of revenue can flow down to earnings. A company usually spend on a few key categories:

a.Cost of Goods Sold ("COGS"): How much does it cost for the company to produce and deliver what it sells? If the company can find ways to optimize production efficiency or negotiate more discounts from suppliers, then COGS will decrease, and EPS will increase.

b.Sales & Marketing: How much does it cost for the company to create demand for what it sells? This cost is spent on sales force, marketing campaigns, etc. If the company can find ways to reduce this spending, then the Sales & Marketing cost will decrease, and EPS will increase.

c.General & Administrative ("G&A"): How much does the company spend on running administrative tasks? This is usually driven by 1) how many employees the company has and 2) how much the company pays these employees. So a company can reduce its G&A cost through layoffs, lower bonuses or salaries, less generous employee benefits and expat packages, etc. It can also outsource some functionalities offshore, where the labor cost is cheaper. This reduces the G&A cost, and increases EPS.

3.Share Count Decrease: A lower share count means the total earnings pool is split up among less shares, so each share gets a great portion of earnings, which means a higher EPS. There's one major way to reduce share count and that's through a Share Repurchase.

a.Share Repurchase: The company can use the cash that it has on its hands to buyback shares from the shareholders. The repurchased shares are retired. So this reduces the number of shares that are out there held by investors. A lower share count = higher EPS.

● What is the significance of "earnings per share"?

Increase in any of the following will push up earnings.

1.Margins of any kind that flows into computation of net income.

2.Efficiency in asset turnover.

3.Increase in leverage because of the tax shield effects.

4.Increases in tax efficiency by loopholes or domicile.

5.Increases in book value from repurchase of stock or increases in retained earnings.

● What Is Earnings Per Share and Why is It Important To Investing?

When a company goes public and starts trading on the stock market, they're obligated to tell investors how they're doing. They can't fudge facts like how much money they made or how profitable they are. Doing so would mean defrauding shareholders, screwing with their share price. They simply need to deliver good or bad news every three months without skipping a beat.

Every quarterly report (or "earnings call") features a slew of crucial data. During these reports, you can find the company's quarterly sales, profit (or loss), expenses, growth percentages, and much more. These data points help investors make informed financial decisions for the future, like buying more stock or selling what they own. They also help analysts predict future quarterly results and what to expect from a company down the line.

Companies also report their earnings per share, an important number that helps investors and analysts alike in charting a company's success. In fact, knowing a company's earnings per share might be one of the most important figures to know about a particular stock, as it could mean great success...or imminent failure.

- What is earnings per share?

A company's earnings per share is a simple way to measure a company's profit. It's calculated by using the following simple equation:earnings per share

A net income (or net profit) is how much money a company made after their costs, operating expenses, and taxes are subtracted from their revenue. For instance, if a company made $90 million in revenue but their taxes and overhead is $80 million, they have a net income of $10 million.A company's outstanding shares are the total shares held by investors. When calculating earnings per share, analysts often use a weighted average of a company's outstanding shares, as that number could change throughout the year.

A dividend is the money paid by a company to its shareholders, usually stemming from their profit. Companies aren't required to pay dividends, though many of them do. They're given to shareholders on a per-share basis at a fixed price. For instance, if a company has 1 million shares and will pay a total of $2 million in dividends, this means each shareholder will get $2 per share. Let's say Company X has a net income of $10 million. They will also pay $2 million in dividends, and have 1 million outstanding shares. How do we calculate that?

earnings per share

Company X has an $8 earnings per share, or EPS. This means that the company is profitable, though how Company X's profitability compares to their last quarter's EPS and their competitors is more important than this single number.

Should you base your investments entirely on a company's EPS?

There are many factors to consider when looking to invest in a company. Earnings per share is just one of them. You can save yourself from making a bad investment by researching things like year-over-year profit/revenue growth and any news that could impact a company's stock price in the future. Simply looking at a company's EPS won't cut it.If you want to get some idea of how a company is performing, look at their EPS and compare it to previous quarters. Then look at what analysts predicted for the company's EPS this quarter and other quarters. If a company continuously outperformed expectations and their EPS grew over the span of a year, that's a pretty good indication of growth. If a company misses expectations and EPS stagnates or shrinks, they might be in for a world of hurt.

Can a company have a negative earnings per share?

Absolutely. Earlier this week, Tesla ($TSLA) announced a quarterly loss for the first three months of 2017. This means that the loss and lack of a dividend divided by the outstanding shares would equal a negative EPS (or -$1.33, in this instance). Tesla's investors and financial analysts didn't expect Tesla to post a positive EPS, as the company only did once in the last few years. At the same time, Tesla still posted a lower earnings per share than analysts expected. This caused the stock to dip by over 5% as of this writing, and Tesla remains unprofitable for the time being.

EPS or Earning per share assist an investor to take an effective investment decision. A high EPS indicates that the company is doing very well in acquiring a good amount of return from each share. A high EPS always attracts more potential investors. This is why calculating EPS of a company before making an investment decision is important.

Earning per share is the profit allocation to every outstanding share attributed in the company.

It is the ratio of total profit less income tax less dividend on preferred stock to the total number of outstanding share.

It is used to calculate P/E of the company. It is equal to current stock price divided by EPS.

P/E measure how much we have to investment to earn 1 rupees.

It is a indicator for company profitability.

One of the most important things investors see it's earnings, because is the amount of money the company generated. But earnings alone doesn't give you that much information, you need to compare it with the size of the company, or the amount you invested in that company.

Lets say you got a one year return of $1,000 on an asset you bought. If you invested $1,000 then is great because you have a 100% in one year. But if you invested $1,000,000 then you only got 0.1%. So, shares purchase number is such as fixed saving amout to bank, if you can buy many shares to invest the company for one year, and you can predict the company's shares prices must increase to the highest level after one year. Then, you must sell your the company's shares to earn the highest profit after one year. So, share purchase number must influence your share earning sale profit. You can not neglect this share purchase number factor.

● Methods of Valuation of Shares

(i) On a going/continuing concern basis; and

(ii) Break-up value basis.

In the case of former, the utility of the assets is to be considered for the purpose of arriving at the value of the assets, but, in the case of the latter, the realizable value of the assets is to be taken. Under this method, value of the net assets of the company is to be determined first.

Thereafter, the net assets are to be divided by the number of shares in order to rind out the value of each share. At the same time, value of goodwill (at its market value), investment (non-trading assets) are to be added to net assets. Similarly, if there are any preference shares, those are also to be deducted with their arrear dividends from the net assets.

However, this following step should carefully be followed while calculating Net Assets or the Funds Available for Equity Shareholders:

(a) Ascertain the total market value of fixed assets and current assets;

(b) Compute the value of goodwill (as per the required method);

(c) Ascertain the total market value of non-trading assets (like investment) which are to be added;

(d) All fictitious assets (viz, Preliminary Expenses, Discount on issue of Shares/Debentures, Debit-Balance of P&L A/c etc.) must be excluded;

(e) Deduct the total amount of Current Liabilities, Amount of Debentures with arrear interest," if any, Preference Share Capital with arrear dividend, if any.

(f) The balance left is called the Net Assets or Funds Available for Equity Shareholders.

Alternatively:

Net Assets = Share Capital + Reserves and Surplus Revaluation – Loss on Revaluation

Applicability of the Method:

(i) The permanent investors determine the value of shares under this method at the time of purchasing the shares;

(ii) The method is particularly applicable when the shares are valued at the time of Amalgamation, Absorption and Liquidation of companies; and

(iii) This method is also applicable when shares are acquired for control motives.

For the purpose of valuing the shares of the company, the assets were revalued as: Goodwill $ 50,000; Land and Building at cost plus 50%, Plant and Machinery $ 1, 00,000; Investments at book values; Stock $80,000 and Debtors at book value, less 10%.

Intrinsic Value of each share = Funds available for Equity Shares/Total Number of Shares

Intrinsic Value of shares = $ 3, 30,000/20,000

= $ 16.50.

Intrinsic Value of Shares on the Basis of Valuation of Goodwill

(a) Land and Building and Plant and Machinery were revalued at$ 15, 00,000 and $2, 28,000, respectively.

(b) Investments were valued at market value.

(c) Stock to be taken at $ 80,000 and Debtors subject to a deduction @ 10% for bad debts.

(d) Net profit (before Tax) for the last five years were: $ 50,000; $ 70,000; $ 80,000; $ 1, 00,000 and $ 1, 25,000.

(e) Managerial Remuneration $ 8,000 to be charged against profit for every year.

(f) Normal Rates of Return 10%.

(g) Goodwill to be valued at 5 years' purchase of Super-Profit.

(h) Rate of tax 50%.

Yield-Basis Method:

Yield is the effective rate of return on investments which is invested by the investors. It is always expressed in terms of percentage. Since the valuation of shares is made on the basis of Yield, it is called Yield-Basis Method. For example, an investor purchases one share of Rs. 100 (face value and paid-up value) at Rs. 150 from a Stock Exchange on which he receives a return (dividend) @ 20%.

(i) Profit Basis;

(ii) Dividend Basis.

(i) Profit Basis:

Under this method, at first, profit should be ascertained on the basis of past average profit; thereafter, capitalized value of profit is to be determined on the basis of normal rate of return, and, the same (capitalized value of profit) is divided by the number of shares in order to find out the value of each share.

The following procedure may be adopted:

Two companies, A Ltd. and B. Ltd., are found to be exactly similar as to their assets, reserves and liabilities except that their share capital structures are different:

The share capital of A. Ltd. is $ 11,00,000, divided into 1,000, 6% Preference Shares of $100 each and 1,00,000 Equity Shares of $ 10 each.

The share capital of B. Ltd. is also $11,00,000, divided into 1,000, 6% Preference Shares of $100 each and 1,00,000 Equity Shares of $ 10 each. .

The fair yield in respect of the Equity Shares of this type of companies is ascertained at 8%.

The profits of the two companies for 2009 are found to be $1, 10,000 and $ 1, 50,000, respectively.

Calculate the value of the Equity Shares of each of these two companies on 31.12.2009 on the basis of this information only. Ignore taxation.

Whether Profit Basis or Dividend Basis method is followed for ascertaining the value of shares depends on the shares that are held by the respective shareholders. In other words, the shareholders holding minimum number of shares (i.e., minority holding) may determine the value of his shares on dividend basis since he has to satisfy himself having the rate of dividend which is recommended by the Board of Directors, i.e., he has no such power to control the affairs of the company.

On the contrary, the shareholders holding maximum number of shares (i.e., majority holding) has got more controlling rights over the affairs of the company including the recommendation for the rate of divided among others. Under the circumstances, valuation of shares should be made on profit basis. In short, Profit Basis should be followed in the case of Majority Holding, and Dividend Basis should be followed in the case of Minority Holding.

Note:

Yield-Basis Method may also be termed as:

Market Value Method; Profit Basis/Income Basis Method;

Earning Capacity Method etc.

Value of share under yield basis:

Fair Value Method:

There are some accountants who do not prefer to use Intrinsic Value or Yield Value for ascertaining the correct value of shares. They, however, prescribe the Fair Value Method which is the mean of Intrinsic Value Method end Yield Value Method. The same provides a better indication about the value of shares than the earlier two methods.

Formula of Fair Value Method

Fair value = (Intrinsic value + yield value) / 2

Ascertain the value of each equity share under Fair Value Method on the basis of the information given:

Assets are revalued as:

Building $3, 20,000, Plant $ 1, 80,000, Stock $ 45,000 and Debtors $36,000. Average Profit of the company is $1, 20,000 and 12½% of profit is transferred to General Reserve, Rate of taxation being 50%. Normal dividend expected on equity shares is 8% whereas fair return on capital employed is 10%. Goodwill may be valued at 3 years' purchase of super-profit.

Return on Capital Employed Method:

Under this method, valuation of share is made on the basis of rate of a return (after tax) on capital employed. Rates of return are taken on the basis of predetermined/ expected rates of return which an investor may expect on the investments. After ascertaining this expected earnings, we are to determine the capital sum for such a return.

Thus, we are to follow the following procedure one by one:

(a) Ascertain the expected (maintainable) profit (after adjustments, if any);

(b) Ascertain the normal rate of return on capital employed for a similar business;

(c) At last, on the basis of expected rate of return, capitalize the (maintainable) profit.

E. Price-Earnings Ratio Method:

We know that it is the ratio which relates the market price of the share to earning per equity share.

price-earn ratio (PE ratio)= market price of a share (MPS)/ earn per share (EPS)

using PE ratio, we can certain the value of share and value of the business help following as below:

value per share= EPS (earn per share) x P/E ratio

valuation of business = total earning x P/E ratio

On conclusion, evaluation of share price changes, we can apply the company past financial performance to calculate ratio changes, asset and liquid captial ability methods in order to evaluate whether the company's share price will rise up or fall down later and making the choice to decide to either buy or sell the company's shares later.

SIX

DISEASE INFLUENCES SHARE PRICE FALLS REASONS

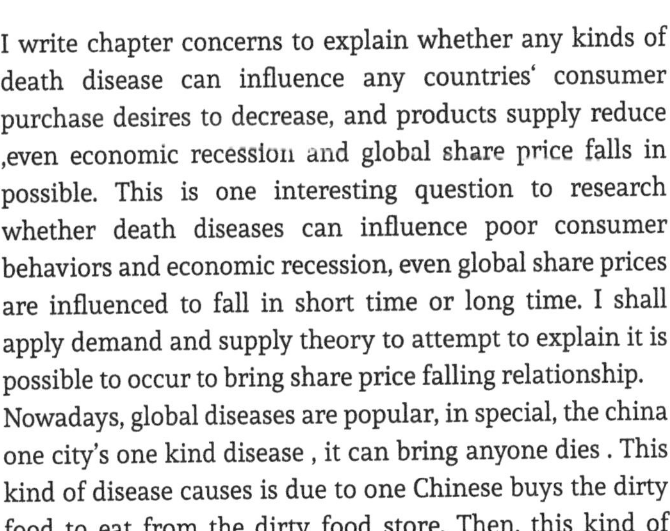

I write chapter concerns to explain whether any kinds of death disease can influence any countries' consumer purchase desires to decrease, and products supply reduce ,even economic recession and global share price falls in possible. This is one interesting question to research whether death diseases can influence poor consumer behaviors and economic recession, even global share prices are influenced to fall in short time or long time. I shall apply demand and supply theory to attempt to explain it is possible to occur to bring share price falling relationship.
Nowadays, global diseases are popular, in special, the china one city's one kind disease , it can bring anyone dies . This kind of disease causes is due to one Chinese buys the dirty food to eat from the dirty food store. Then, this kind of

disease causes his lung is hurt, then he contact any chinese to get this kinds of diseases. However, this kind of disease brings many people die in China, even these disease Chinese leave China to fly to any where, e.g. US, UK, Hong Kong, Korea, Japan etc. countries. So, this kind of disease will cause many different countries people die in possible.

I shall apply economic theory to explain how pollution causes death diseases to influence food demand (environment protection to provide fresh food demand) and food supply (polluted food or non-polluted food market) change to any countries' food market in either polluted or non-polluted food market environments.

Infectious diseases emerging throughout history have included some of the most feared plagues of the past. New infections continue to emerge today, while many of the old plagues are with us still. These are global problems (William Foege, former CDC director now at the Carter Center, terms them global infectious disease threats). As demonstrated by influenza epidemics, under suitable circumstances, a new infection first appearing anywhere in the world could traverse entire continents within days or weeks.

"Emerging" infectious diseases can be defined as infections that have newly appeared in a population or have existed but are rapidly increasing in incidence or geographic range. Among recent examples are HIV/AIDS, hantavirus pulmonary syndrome, Lyme disease, and hemolytic uremic syndrome (a foodborne infection caused by certain strains of Escherichia coli). Specific factors precipitating disease emergence can be identified in virtually all cases. These include ecological, environmental, or demographic factors that place people at increased contact with a previously unfamiliar microbe or its natural host or promote dissemination. These factors are increasing in prevalence;

this increase, together with the ongoing evolution of viral and microbial variants and selection for drug resistance, suggests that infections will continue to emerge and probably increase and emphasizes the urgent need for effective surveillance and control.

We can define as emerging infections that have newly appeared in the population, or have existed but are rapidly increasing in incidence or geographic range (1,2). Recent examples of emerging diseases in various parts of the world include HIV/AIDS; classic cholera in South America and Africa; cholera due to Vibrio cholerae O139; Rift Valley fever; hantavirus pulmonary syndrome; Lyme disease

Can disease sick influence global share price fall in possible? I believe that disease sick has indirect relationship to cause global share market price falls. The question concerns whether the firm share price can fall how much and the firm's share price need to fall how long and what the firm's share price is the lowest falling down. However, when one kind of disease sick , it can be delivered to cause this kind of disease by mouth, or body contract method and this kind of disease sick can cause anyone die. Then, it will cause threat to anyone to leave their homes easily. For example, China is encoutering this kind of disease sick, it can cause many Chinese are fear to leave homes. So, it means that any shops will have less number of customers to visit as well as any product manufacturers won't need their factory workers to go to factories to work because they are fear to be caused this kind of disease sick to bring death risk.

So, on poor customer demand view, Chinese consumers number reduces because they spend less time to visit any shops to choose any products to buy . Consequently any products demand will decrease in China. Moreover, many

Chinese go to other countries in this disease sick period, because some of Chinese have this kind of disease sick, they will contact the country's people. Then, the disease sick Chinese will contact them to bring disease sick to deliver to the country's people. For example, US, UK, Korea, Singapore , Hong Kong etc. countries. Then, this kind of disease sick will influence the these countries people feel fear to leave their home to avoid to get this kind of disease sick to cause death by mouth, hand, air contact on streets. Then, it also bring less people spend much time to visit any shops when they spend much time to stay at home. It means that consumption chance will also reduce or customer purchase demand will increase. On poor supply view, when firms feel employees safety in this kind of disease sick time, they will force employees to stay at homes to avoid disease sick delivered chance when they need to contact to work. So, employers won't need pay much wages to employees because they do not need to go to factories to work or fires some workers. Consequently, any products manufacturing number must reduce as well as products supply will also reduce. If this disease sick is staying to the country , such as China, Hong Kong, Korea etc. in long time. Then, it will cause supply to any products shortage challenge as well as reducing customer demand to purchase product challenge in the same time.

The question is: Why and how can this reducing supply to products number and reducing demand to product purchase issue influence share market share falls ? Have they bring cause and effect relationship between them? I shall explain the reasons as below:

Stock prices tick up and down constantly due to fluctuations in supply and demand. If more people want to buy a stock, its market price will increase. If more people are trying to sell a stock, its price will fall. The relationship between supply and demand is highly sensitive to the news of the moment. Nonetheless, chasing the news is not a good stock-picking strategy for the individual investor. In most cases, professional traders react in anticipation of an event, not when the event is reported. Human disease attack is one kind of indirect relationship to influence consumers' visiting shops time to be reduced , due to they are fear to leave homes if the kind of disease sick can kill any people when they are walking to be delivered this kind of disease from anyone on streets. So, when the country has many people are delivered this kind of disease which can kill anyone. It can cause people choose to stay at home long time. So, visiting shops time is also influenced to reduce. It is one cause and effect relationship issue. When shops have less customers, then purchase demand is also influenced to reduce and sale of product number will also decrease. Also, when one country existens death disease attack, then many people will lose jobs because employers feel they do not need many workers to work in the death disease occurrence time. Economic recession will occur in this death disease occurrence time to any countries.

- Emerging infectious diseases and share market relationship

(1) Can emerging infectious diseases influence share market price falls in agriculture market? I believe that food business , e.g. some supermarket share price will be influenced to fallen down. Infectious diseases are emerging globally at an unprecedented rate while global food demand is projected to increase sharply by 2100. Here, we synthesize the pathways by which projected agricultural expansion and intensification will influence human

infectious diseases and how human infectious diseases might likewise affect food production and distribution. Feeding 11 billion people will require substantial increases in crop and animal production that will expand agricultural use of antibiotics, water, pesticides and fertilizer, and contact rates between humans and both wild and domestic animals, all with consequences for the emergence and spread of infectious agents. Indeed, our synthesis of the literature suggests that, since 1940, agricultural drivers were associated with >25% of all — and >50% of zoonotic — infectious diseases that emerged in humans, proportions that will likely increase as agriculture expands and intensifies. We identify agricultural and disease management and policy actions, and additional research, needed to address the public health challenge posed by feeding 11 billion people. So, scientists ensure that infectious diseases can be caused when the person buys dirty food to eat from the food shop. If one large supermarket, it neglects to sell some or many dirty foods, e.g. pork, beef meats to let many people to eat. After if the country has some people are confimed that they are attacked by infectious diseases , due to they bought the infectious diseases meats to eat from the supermarket. Consequently, when this bad news are known by television or radio or newspaper public channels. Many people are fear to eat infectious diseases foods from this supermarket. So, there are many meat consumers will choose other supermarkets to replace this supermarket to buy meat to eat. In the result, I believe that this supermarket share price will fall down as well as when its share price will rise , it depends on when there are none people have infectious diseases in the country. So, this infectious diseases may have indirect relationship to bring this supermarket share price to be reduced because share investors will lose confidence to buy this supermarket shares, they believe that its beef or any kinds of meat will have infectious diseases , so it will lose many food consumers choose to buy its meat to eat.

The human population is growing, requiring more space for food production, and needing more animals to feed it. Emerging infectious diseases are increasing, causing losses in both human and animal lives, as well as large costs to society. Many factors are contributing to disease emergence, including climate change, globalization and urbanization, and most of these factors are to some extent caused by humans. The climate-sensitive vector-borne diseases are likely to be emerging due to climate changes and environmental changes, such as increased irrigation. The anthropogenic changes contributing to disease emergence are described, as well as how they directly and indirectly cause either increased numbers of susceptible or exposed individuals, or cause increased infectivity. Many actions may have multiple direct or indirect effects, and it may be difficult to assess what the consequences may be. In addition, most anthropogenic drivers are related to desired activities, such as logging, irrigation, trade, and travelling, which the society is requiring. It is important to research more about the indirect and direct effects of the different actions to understand both the benefits and the risks. So, in our business environment, emerging infectious diseases will bring indirect negative influence to any kinds of businesses' share prices to fall down in possible. For agricultural market example, when the country has many people have infectious diseases and they are confirmed that they are eaten infectious diseases food, but if they do not know whether they buy the infectious diseases food from which shops. Then, in macro economic negative view, the country's overall agricultural market share price will reduce because overseas meat food consumers will feel fear to buy the county's meat or vegetable to eat , due to infectious diseases food supply may export to themselve country. So, this country's agricultural meat or vegetable export may be influenced to reduce number to any countries because export food demand number may be influenced to reduce due to infectious diseases food attack to this country in this period. So, overall this country's agricultural market share price may be influenced to go down in possible in this time. Unless, when this country has none people are confirmed to eat infectious diseases food to be dead, then this country's agricultural market share price may rise up because many overseas food consumers believe it has none any infectious diseases food existen . So they have confidence to eat this country any kinds of agricultural food and this country's overall agricultural food export number will rise. Many investors have confidence to buy shares to invest this country's any supermarkets, food stores, restaurants etc. different food businesses. Hence, it seems that infectious diseases can bring some food business share price goes down in possible.

(2) Can infectious diseases influence travel market share price to be fallen down?

Travel is a potent force in the emergence of disease. Migration of humans has been the pathway for disseminating infectious diseases throughout recorded history and will continue to shape the emergence, frequency, and spread of infections in geographic areas and populations. The current volume, speed, and reach of travel are unprecedented. The consequences of travel extend beyond the traveler to the population visited and the ecosystem. When they travel, humans carry their genetic makeup, immunologic sequelae of past infections, cultural preferences, customs, and behavioral patterns. Microbes, animals, and other biologic life also accompany them.

Today's massive movement of humans and materials sets the stage for mixing diverse genetic pools at rates and in combinations previously unknown. Concomitant changes in the environment, climate, technology, land use, human behavior, and demographics converge to favor the emergence of infectious diseases caused by a broad range of organisms in humans, as well as in plants and animals. Many factors contribute to the emergence of infectious diseases. Those frequently identified include microbial adaptation and change, human demographics and behavior, environmental changes, technology and economic development, breakdown in public health measures and surveillance, and international travel and commerce. So, it may bring this question: Can the emergence of infectious diseases occur to the country , it can influence many travellers choose to go to the country to travel and it can bring investors lose confidence to invest to the country's hotel, airline etc. tourism service industries to cause share pricc reduces.

Travel is a potent force in disease emergence and spread. The current volume, speed, and reach of travel are unprecedented. The consequences of migration extend beyond the traveler to the population visited and the ecosystem . Travel and trade set the stage for mixing diverse genetic pools at rates and in combinations previously unknown. Massive movement and other concomitant changes in social, political, climatic, environmental, and technologic factors converge to favor the emergence of infectious diseases.

Disease emergence is complex. Often several events must occur simultaneously or sequentially for a disease to emerge or reemerge. Travel allows a potentially pathogenic microbe to be introduced into a new geographic area; however, to be established and cause disease a microbe must survive, proliferate, and find a way to enter a susceptible host. Any analysis of emergence must look at a dynamic process, a sequence of events, a milieu, or ecosystem. Movement, changing patterns of resistance and vulnerability, and the emergence of infectious diseases also affect plants, animals, and insect vectors. Analysis of these species can hold important lessons about the dynamics of human disease.

To assess the impact of travel on disease emergence, it is necessary to consider the receptivity of a geographic area and its population to microbial introduction. Most introductions do not lead to disease. Organisms that survive primarily or entirely in the human host and are spread through sexual contact, droplet nuclei, and close physical contact can be readily carried to any part of the world. For example, AIDS, tuberculosis, measles, pertussis, diphtheria, and hepatitis B are easily carried by travelers and can spread in a new geographic area; however, populations protected by vaccines resist introduction. Organisms that have animal hosts, environmental limitations, arthropod vectors, or complicated life cycles become successively more difficult to "transplant" to another geographic area or population. Epidemics of dengue fever and yellow fever cannot appear in a geographic area unless competent mosquito vectors are present. Schistosomiasis cannot spread in an environment unless a suitable snail intermediate host exists in that region. Organisms that survive only under carefully tuned local conditions are less likely to be successfully introduced. Even if an introduced parasite persists in a new geographic area, it does not necessarily cause human disease. In the United States, humans infected with Taenia solium, the parasite that causes cysticercosis, infrequently transmit the infection because sanitary disposal of feces, the source of the eggs, is generally available. In short, the likelihood of transmission involves many biological, social, and environmental variables.

Hence, when one country is confirmed that it has disease emergence in its society. Then, it will cause many people are fear to live hotels or catch air planes to fly to this country to travel in this time. When this country has many travellers decide to choose other countries to travel. It implies that its overall tourism business, such as living hotels needs will reduce and catching air planes to this country travel needs will also reduce. So, investors will lose confidence to buy this country's any tourism industry hotels shares or restaurant shares or airlines shares in this time. Consequently, this country's time airline and hotel and restaurant share prices will be influenced to reduce.

On conclusion, I beleive that when disease emergence occurrence to any country, it will influence some kinds of businesses shares prices to be go down, in especial, in tourism and agricultural industry. So, disease emergence occurrence to any countries may have indirect negative factor to influence the countries' overall agricultural and/or tourism markets shares prices to be fallen down in possible.

9 798887 497150

Printed by Libri Plureos GmbH in Hamburg,
Germany